THE BEGINN

SEO

How to **Optimize Your Website,
Rank Higher on Google** and **Drive More Traffic**

JESSICA AINSWORTH

The Beginners'Guide to SEO
Copyright © 2021 by Jessica Ainsworth

Author photo by Todd I. Mason, Jr.,
                    Capture Essence Photography
Cover Design by 100 Covers
Formatting & Typesetting by Black Bee Media

ISBN: 978-1-7356885-8-9 (Paperback)
       978-1-7356885-7-2 (Ebook)

Acknowledgements

Well, it looks like writing books is like the Pringles slogan: "once you pop you just can't stop." So, here we are again. Whether you're just discovering this book and my series or if you've read any of my books before this, I thank you for your support!

To my husband who has put up with my antics while writing this book and for being my partner in all things, thank you. A big thanks to my kids as well who have had to sacrifice some time for me to finish this book and for their continued love and support.

I'm a fan of the saying "it takes a village" because it does in fact, take a village… Thank you to my village for supporting me and helping me: Sherry, Bob & Aislinn; Rob & Jessica; Patty & Alex; Tony.

Thanks to my professional village: Steve & Jyllian; Joris; and Arjen plus the SPS community!! I sincerely appreciate the mentorship, the help, last minute requests and calming of panic!!

A big thank you to SEMrush for allowing me to use some of their infographics in my book! Not only do they have some pretty awesome infographics and articles, they also have a tool sure to wow any SEO - whether you're just beginning, an intermediate or even advanced in your knowledge. No, they did not ask me to put that in there and no, I am not receiving a commission for that. They're just that awesome.

Free Resources

I've put together a collection of some free resources to help you take your SEO strategy further. From templates to worksheets and infographics, you'll find a ton of resources to help you take the next step. To access your free resources, follow the link below.

Download your FREE resources here:

https://beginnersguidetomarketing.com/seo

For even more resources pertaining to SEO and marketing as a whole, check out my Patreon page:

https://www.patreon.com/beginnersguidetomarketing

Table of Contents

Part III: Technical SEO

Part IV: The Extra Bits

Introduction

If you're reading this book, chances are you've at least heard the term SEO in passing. If you haven't don't worry, we'll cover it in depth as we go along. This book is designed for beginners and is not meant to make you a subject matter expert. What this book *does* do is provide a basic understanding of what the elements consist of, why they're important and provides a basic level break down of how to accomplish the task.

When done *correctly*, SEO can help you rank on page one of Google and the other search engines. This is not just for vanity, but rather the amount of traffic you bring to your website. Ranking on page one is not easy and it will take time and hard work, but once you're there, you'll be glad you spent the time and effort on it. More traffic means more conversions.

Have you heard of the joke "Where's the best place to hide a dead body? Page 2 of Google."? It's a joke that is both funny and bittersweet. When querying the search engines, many do not venture past page one and the few that go past to page two, usually don't go farther than there. Though there are exceptions, they are few in numbers. Ranking on page one can greatly increase your visibility and drive significantly more traffic to your website, depending on the words you're ranking for.

And it's not just about using the right keywords, there are over 200 factors that go into determining where Google and the other search engines will rank you.

But what even is SEO?

What is SEO?

SEO stands for Search Engine Optimization and it is the process of optimizing your website to rank higher on the search engines - like Google. Google has an algorithm with **over 200** ranking factors - some of which is known, some of which is not. You see, Google, like many tech companies, isn't willing to share the secret sauce with the world, and who can blame them?! If we all knew what those 200 ranking factors were, it would turn into a soup sandwich pretty freaking fast.

As the economy and technology both continue to grow, change is inevitable and Google's algorithm changes just as often. Sometimes we get advanced warning and other times, you find out when your rank experiences a HUGE decline. As of right now, we know that Google will be rolling out a pretty big algorithm update called the Page Experience in 2021. They gave us all several months' worth of notice, which is rarely the case. Maybe they're taking pity on us due to COVID-19's impact.

I digress…

The Page Experience update will have shaken many businesses, really those who have not bothered to take heed to Google's warning. Here's what it comes down to. Yes, you need to make sure your SEO is in tip top condition, and a part of that is focusing on the User Experience (UX). If users aren't happy with the look or feel or wording of your website, they'll leave as soon as they get there. This sends a message to Google that maybe your website isn't as relevant to users and perhaps you should rank a bit lower, making way for websites that *are* more relevant.

Comprised of three key parts, SEO is made up of:

1. On-Site SEO (on your website)

2. Off-Site SEO (off of your website directing back to your website)

3. Technical SEO (the super nerdy stuff - brace yourself)

Another aspect of SEO is *local SEO*, but that will come under off-site SEO, so hold tight. Just so I don't confuse you before we even start this journey, let's quickly run through those four.

On-site SEO is the optimization on your website. There's a lot that goes on behind the scenes of websites. When you google your website, you'll notice that it shows up in a particular way. When your URL in and visit your own website, you may have set the image to show in the tab (favicon is what it's called) and there should be some text there. That text, the way you show on Google, those are all things that can be optimized.

Off-site SEO is the optimization of your website through *other* websites. It is conducted *off* of your website. A big part of proving that your website is trustworthy to search engines like Google is done through backlinks. Backlinks are links on other people's websites that link to your website. Another element to off-site SEO is *local SEO*. Local SEO is a form of off-site SEO used to help boost your ranking *in your local area.* This means that you may rank higher when someone is looking for your services in your geographic location, *not* that you would rank higher nationally or globally for the term.

Technical SEO is technical and nerdy and is conducted on your website. From ensuring that you have a SEO friendly URL to fixing broken links (links that no longer work on your website) and about much more. I'd mention them, but I don't want to scare you off…. When you get to that chapter, we'll walk through what it is and how to piece it together in a way that is hopefully broken down enough that even beginner's can understand it. Because that's who this book is written for.

Resources at a Glance

At the end of this book you'll find a step by step guide to running an SEO audit. Once you've read the book and have a good understanding of what you're getting into, I'd recommend that you run an audit on your website to see where you can make some improvements.

To further help you along your SEO journey, I've created a Facebook Group: Beginner's Guide to SEO. This group is designed to help answer any questions you may have. Additionally, feel free to reach out if you think there's something missing or could be expanded on a bit more in this book. This book is intended to be a living document and updated annually. Algorithms and methodology change way too often for this book to be the end all be all of SEO, and it's certainly not intended to be that either. It is simply for *beginners* who need help understanding the terminology and how to get started.

https://www.facebook.com/groups/beginnersguidetoseo

Like my other books, I've also created some worksheets, infographics and other useful bits of information that you can download *for free* by visiting:

https://beginnersguidetomarketing.com/seo

Finally, yet *another* resource to help you continue learning more about SEO and marketing as a whole, subscribe to my podcast!

https://anchor.fm/jessica-ainsworth

Enough with the resources and semi-promotion here, and on to the meat and potatoes. There will be plenty more resources of a much broader nature at the end of the book spanning the tools and resources we mention as you go along.

You're about to embark on a journey that is both challenging and rewarding. If you stick with it and let us know in the group if you get stuck with anything, your SEO will be much better for it.

All right. Take a deep breath and let's get to it.

SEO v. PPC: What's the Difference?

If you're wondering what the difference between SEO and PPC is, don't worry, you're not alone. What it all boils down to is how to get your website to rank on page one for certain keywords when users query search engines like Google. The main difference here is that one is *paid* while the other is *organic*. To really understand the significance of either, let's look at *why* you should be working towards the coveted first page on Google.

Aiming for Page One Rank on Google

Have you ever heard the saying "Where's the best place to hide a dead body? The second page of Google…"?

Nerdy, I know, but it still brings an element of truth. There are over 6+ billion searches on Google *every single day*. From all of those people querying Google, a whopping 75% will **not** go past the first page on a Google Search. So, if you're ranking on page two or worse yet, page three or four, you're missing out on an enormous amount of potential traffic to your website and ultimately, paying customers.

At this point, you may be wondering still *why* you should care about ranking on page one, so here's another statistic that can help you see the light… Approximately 93% of online experiences begin with a search engine. That's right, 93% of online experiences begin with an individual querying Google or another search engine.

How to Rank on Page One

There are essentially two ways to rank on the search engine: paid and organic. When we say paid, we don't mean that you can pay to rank on the first page in terms of SEO; We mean that you can pay to have an advertisement shown on page one of a user's search results for specific keywords. Have you ever queried Google for something and noticed that the first few and the last couple of results on that page have the word "Ad" in there? That is a PPC (pay per click) advertisement. The remainder of the results that do not have the word *Ad* in front of it is an organic result and those ranking on page one would have gotten to page one through their SEO efforts.

What is SEO?

SEO stands for Search Engine Optimization and it is both an art and science. SEO can be broken down into three parts:

1. On-Site SEO
2. Off-Site SEO
3. Technical SEO

On-Site SEO

Just like the name implies, on-site SEO is SEO *on your website*. From optimizing your heading tags to help Google's search bots (and the other search engine's bots) crawl and index your website to keyword optimization to help the right people find your website, on-site SEO (like all other types of SEO) is a critical piece to your company's digital success.

You did not wake up today to be mediocre.

Off-Site SEO

As the term on-site has to deal with *on your website*, off-site SEO is a form of SEO that is conducted *off of your website.* A big piece to the SEO puzzle consists of backlinks and inbound marketing. These links demonstrate to Google and the other search engines that your website is both credible and authoritative, leading them to rank your site higher.

Bear in mind that Google aims to provide optimal *user experiences* and so, if they're not sure that you're credible or authoritative, they may not rank your content as high in the search results.

A part of your off-site SEO will also consist of building your *local SEO*. Local SEO is when you go out and get your website listed in relevant directories. This can help improve your search engine rankings *in your local area*. A lot of those links from the directories will prove beneficial to your Domain Authority.

Domain Authority (DA) is a term created by a company called Moz. They created a way for users to see where their website's DA **might be so they can identify areas that need to be improved on. The higher your Domain Authority, the more credible and authoritative your website is - in theory.*

The caveat to off-site SEO here is that you should avoid any black hat link building tactics such as link farming and more. If you were to pay spammy websites for links back to your own site, Google may not see your site as quality based on the poor quality of the sites linking back to you.

If you're going to do something, isn't it worth doing right the first time?

Technical SEO

Technical SEO is a beast. For those outside of the SEO industry, technical SEO can seem very intimidating leading many to outsource their SEO to skilled agencies. Some things included in technical SEO include schema markup, meta tags and canonicalization to name a few. Technical SEO is just as important as on-site and off-site SEO and should not be passed over simply because it's intimidating.

What is PPC?

PPC stands for Pay Per Click and it literally means that you pay each time someone clicks on your advertisement. Did you catch that last word there? Advertisement…

That's right, PPC is placing an advertisement to target a specific target audience querying specific keywords. When doing some competitive or keyword research you may see that some keywords have a CPC (cost per click) number next to the keyword. That CPC is the cost of each click on your advertisement. So, the higher the number, the more you'll pay. If you're working with a lower budget, you'll want to target those long tail keywords and not broad phrases to get the most bang for your buck.

What's the Difference Between SEO and PPC?

The short version is that PPC is a paid way of showing your

website in the coveted top positions on Google (and the other search engines). SEO is a way of *organically* ranking on page one, meaning you can't pay for that position, but rather, you must put in work to gain the top spot.

SEO takes time and a long-haul effort that can bring long-term results. It can take 4 to 6 months to really start seeing results if you're working on your SEO game consistently. The important part to remember here is that SEO is not a one and done type of thing but must be continually built upon. The moment you grow stagnant in your efforts is the very same moment your competition will strike and overtake you.

PPC however, offers the benefit of creating laser-targeted visibility in that your advertisements are shown to your target audience (those who are more likely to convert).

It's important to note that SEO and PPC are vastly different and do not impact each other either negatively or positively. You cannot pay for *organic* ranking, which is where SEO comes in. Google wants to ensure that they are providing the best possible results to their users who are querying the search engine. If you were able to pay to be displayed instead of working on SEO, the results would be very off kilter and the user experience would not be ideal. So, Google therefore, looking to provide optimal user experiences, will rank websites based on their SEO. They do, however, allow advertisers to pay for advertisements to be shown to those querying the search engines (which is how Google makes their money).

Should You Invest in SEO or PPC?

While your budget may be the determining factor here,

SEO is critical to your company's digital success. Without it, you may as well be invisible.

With that being said, why not consider both?

If you're looking to improve your SEO and you know that it's a long-haul effort that takes time, you could always run PPC ads to supplement your traffic while you're waiting for SEO take come in and build up to rank on page one.

And even after you rank on page one, by combining your SEO efforts with PPC ads, you can maximize your visibility and clicks to drive *even more* traffic your way. While they don't *have to* be run together, they do help you to become a formidable digital force.

Regardless of the direction you choose, SEO is vital and should not be completely passed over forever. It's understandable if you're working with a limited budget that you may need to focus on one over the other, but when your budget allows, you should absolutely without a doubt work on your website's SEO. And hey, if time is what's holding your SEO up, you could always outsource it to agencies such as Pendragon Consulting. Whether you're just looking to learn or want someone to do it for you, we've got you covered.

Search Engine Marketing (SEM)

Yet another term for you to learn! SEM stands for Search Engine Marketing. Don't worry, it's not as confusing as it sounds. In fact, you've already learned about it just moments ago. SEM is just another way of saying paid advertising on search engine platforms such as Google.

Part I

On-Site SEO

On-Site SEO

On-site SEO is made up of all the optimization __on__ your website. This includes the following:

- Meta tags
- Meta descriptions
- Image optimization
- Heading tags
- Internal links
- Keyword research
- Blogging

Don't worry, we'll be covering all that and more over the next few chapters.

Here's some quick Q&A's to get the *on-site SEO* ball rolling.

Why are Keywords Important?

Keywords are the words or phrases that indicate what your website is about. These are the search terms you want to be found for when somebody types in a search query in their browser bar or asks Google Home or Alexa a question.

Keywords are broad terms. Key phrases are also called long-tail keywords. A key phrase is a grouping of two or more words that offer a specific idea. An example of a keyword vs. a key phrase would be "locksmith vs. locksmith in Chattanooga."

Broad keywords are important, but much harder to rank for when you're a small or new business. It's often advised to target keywords with search intent or long-tail phrases. Another example would be "snorkeling vs.

How can I learn to snorkel?" In the second example, you can see the intent of the question. The first phrase would pull in multiple topics: snorkeling as a hobby, gear, places to snorkel, and more. If you're a small shop that teaches snorkeling lessons, the second phrase is specific and helpful. By creating groups of keywords that are specific to your website, you'll have a better chance of sending the right kind of signals to Google, so that you'll show up higher in search rankings.

What are Meta Tags or Meta Descriptions?
Meta tags or descriptions are tags that are coded into your site that tell search engines what your site or individual page is about. Going with the locksmith example above, you'd want to narrow down to what you do and where you do it. Your meta tags would indicate not only that you're a locksmith, but most likely the services you offer and your location. Your description is a short blurb that describes what your page is about. These are like little red flags you're waving, telling search engines like Google, that these are important keywords and ideas that represent your site.

What are Header Tags?
Notice the phrase directly above this sentence. "What are header tags?" When you emphasize a phrase by using header tags with proper code, it says this segment is an important indicator of what is on this particular page of my website. Note the headers in this article. We're highlighting important sections, separating them into headers so you can easily tell what each part of the article is about, and that if scanning the page, you'd see the overall topic based on the grouping of headers.

What are Alt Tags?

Alt tags is a fancy way to say, the words we use to describe the images on the page. If there is a picture in the middle of your web content, alt tags are another way to indicate to Google and other search engines that you are a good match for the searcher's query. This helps push your site higher. But there's another reason we use alt tags as well.

When you describe what your picture is in an alt tag, it helps those people with visual issues, by telling them what the picture is about. Some web users need a page read to them, due to their vision problem, and this helps your page with accessibility. Alt tags are a great place to use keywords and key phrases in your description. It's another opportunity to emphasize what your website is all about.

How can blogging help you rank higher?

It's no secret that Google likes fresh content. They like relevant content. They like useful content. When you blog, it gives you an opportunity to first, show Google that your site is current. Next, relevant and helpful content are both indicators that you're a quality site that they should trust.

This means that when somebody does a search query for the keywords you rank for; they push you up higher in the rankings. You've created a trustworthy and authoritative site on your niche.

Now that you know the important pieces of on-page SEO and how blogging can help, what will you do first to improve your rankings?

Keyword Research

What is Keyword Research?

Keyword research is both an art and a science. It is an SEO task that involves conducting research to find out what keywords and phrases people are using to query the search engines. Understanding what keywords people are using to find businesses in your industry can help you rank higher in the search engines. Keyword research provides marketers a better understanding of how low or high the demand is for specific keywords and how tough it will be to compete for those words in the *organic* search results while offering some direction to the optimization efforts.

There are two ways to rank on the search engines: organically and through paid advertising. When querying Google for a topic such as "keyword research" like in the image below, you'll notice that the very first result you'll see the word "Ad" before the URL. That means that to get that top spot on your search results, an advertiser paid Google Ads to have it displayed. Sometimes, there will be more than one "Ad" result. Those top results *after* the paid advertisements, are *organic* results. Organic means that the search engine (Google in this case) has determined that it is the closest possible match to your query. It's important to note that keywords are not enough to rank on the search engines, but without it your ranking efforts would be futile. If your results are not relevant to what people are querying, you'll not rank well.

Many individuals do not move past the first page of

search results and those that do, they do not generally go past the third page. Those listed in the top results have an increased amount of traffic to their website, meaning quite a bit more organic exposure to a wider audience.

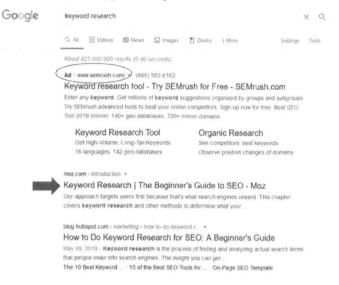

Keyword research is about validating how many searches a specific keyword has. Still, it also allows the exploration of many different ways individuals use language to search for a topic or idea. Thus, keyword researching is not just a crucial part of SEO but also a vital element of content marketing.

It can help marketers find ideas for their next article or blog post, learn about their target audience's needs, and keep up with the lingo of the always-evolving digital landscape. Ultimately, looking for keywords that people mostly use on search engines can help to create targeted content to drive the right traffic to your website and optimize the conversion rate.

The Value and Importance of Keyword Research

Although using keywords that exactly match an individual's search is no longer the most critical ranking factor, according to an SEO professional. But that does not mean that keyword research is an outdated and incompetent process.

Keyword research tells marketers what things or topics people care about and how trendy they actually are among their target audience. By researching keywords that receive a high volume of searches, marketers can identify and sort their content into topics that they want to build content on.

By researching keywords for their search volume, popularity, and general intent, marketers can tackle the questions that most people in their audience want answers to.

If you're new to keyword research and are wondering how to determine the value of your keyword; several tools can help you solve this concern and allow you to make great additions to your keyword research arsenal:

Google Keyword Planner

Google's AdWords Keyword Planner has been one of the most common starting points for SEO keyword research. Nonetheless, Keyword Planner limits search volume data by amalgamating keywords together into huge search volume range buckets.

Google Trends

Google's keyword trend is an excellent tool for discovering seasonal keyword fluctuations. For example, ''delicious thanksgiving recipes will peak in the weeks before Thanksgiving.

Moz Keyword Explorer

Moz's keyword explorer is great for finding keywords that generate a significant amount of traffic, and what makes it more unique is that it's smart! It gives you outside of the box suggestions that you probably won't find anywhere else.

These are a few of the many tools that can help you determine and achieve high-value keywords to rank on search engines.

Surfer's Keyword Surfer

Not as well-known as the others, Keyword Surfer is a Chrome extension that you can install on your Chrome browser. When querying Google, the extension shows you an approximate number of search results and how much it might *cost per click* if running an advertisement with Google Ads for those keywords. In addition to that, it also shows you some other suggested keywords and best of all, a correlation chart showing you things like how many words the article containing those keywords in the top results of the search engine have, how much traffic those pages get, and how many keywords. Take a look below:

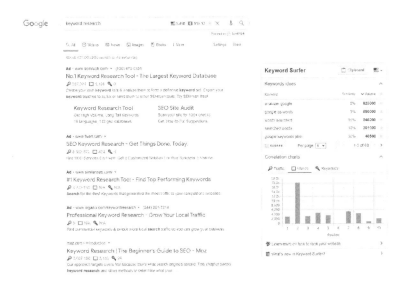

If you're new to keyword research and don't want to pay someone, this tool is a must. You type in the keywords you're targeting, and it tells you what keywords your blog should have, how many times each keyword should be used, how many words it should have, and more. After you've published your content (and it's been indexed by Google) you can go back into Surfer to see how your content ranks, what your competitors for the coveted top spots are doing, and best of all, tips on how to get your content to rank higher (i.e. more of X keywords, increase of word count, backlinks, etc.).

The Keyword Surfer extension is not meant to be an end all, be all for keyword research, but rather to provide a quick snapshot overview - for free.

Benefits of Keyword Research for SEO and Small Businesses

People demand ease and convenience in all aspects of their lives, especially when it comes to online research. Several research shows that <u>seventy-five</u> percent of online users do not even scroll past the first page of search results. This makes it a challenge for businesses to get their content seen and makes it difficult to succeed in search engine optimization efforts.

Several people believe that researching keywords is just a tool for SEO, but small businesses can avail numerous benefits through this approach. New or small businesses do not generally have a considerable amount of money lying around to spend on marketing endeavors like big, well-established companies.

Therefore, using keyword research can help small businesses to rank on search engines, but it is also a very inexpensive means to achieve marketing goals. Few of the many benefits of keyword research for small businesses and SEO are:

Audience Engagement

By developing relevant and high-quality content, businesses can ensure that their audience is engaged with the content and ultimately result in higher ranks on search engines. Audience engagement ensures that visitors keep coming back to your webpage for future reference, resulting in more views and prospects.

Quality Traffic and Conversions

Creating relevant and meaningful content will allow

businesses to attract the right kind of traffic to their webpages and increase the possibility of conversions. This factor is crucial for new or small startups to attract more audience to their brands.

Save Time

Using the correct keywords will allow businesses to save a considerable amount of time and effort. Developing content with the right keywords will not only ensure visibility but will also help to attract new customers. The lack of keyword research can make your content get lost in a sea full of other results, which is only a waste of time and effort.

How to Conduct Keyword Research?

Step 1: Make a list

The first step of this process is to come up with a list of relevant and essential topics related to your business and then use those topics to come up with a few specific keywords further in the process.

The best thing you can do is to put yourself in the shoes of your target audience and think about what topics they would be interested in searching about. This is not your final topic list but rather a big dump of possible key phrases that will ultimately be cropped to a manageable group.

Step 2: Brainstorm

Brainstorming is an integral part of this process and a great way to develop brilliant ideas for keyword research.

Ask yourself similar questions during this step:

- What questions do customers ask?
- How do they talk about their problems?
- What were they searching for when they bumped into you?
- Which of your services or products is most profitable?

The more questions you ask yourself, the better will be the final results.

Step 3: Turn to Forums and Boards

Almost every company has active forums and bulletin boards that folks turn to in search of conversation and information. It is amazing what marketers can find in these places. Such platforms are an excellent place to spot emerging trends and recurring themes.

Simply search for a 'key term + board' or 'key term + forum,' and you will most likely find something related to your business. Moreover, you can head to Wikipedia, search a few key terms, and pay special attention to the table of contents of the search result to find terms you would never have considered otherwise.

If you're looking at a specific forum, board or other website you search for the specific keyword and website using this in Google "site: keyword or phrase + board/forum/website name".

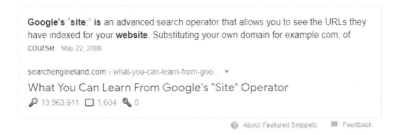

For example, let's say we're looking for something relating to the latest Facebook algorithm update by our favorite marketing guru Pendragon Consulting, LLC. Our query and results might look something like this:

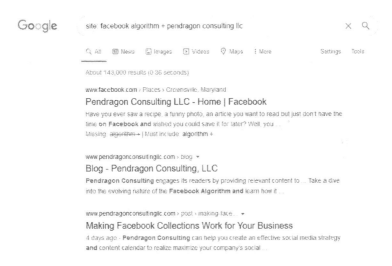

Step 4: Auto-Suggest and Related Terms

The next step is to take a few of the terms to Google and enter them into the search box. Once you begin typing, you may observe that Google starts auto-suggesting terms related to what you are entering. This is a reliable signal by

Google that those terms are popular terms related to what you're searching for. Use these suggestions to expand your list and go through the related searches found on the bottom of the page to get good ideas.

For example, if we were to scroll to the bottom of our query of Google for "keyword research" these terms appear at the bottom. Those are great to help you in terms of keyword research.

Searches related to keyword research

keyword research **tools**	keyword research **meaning**
keyword research **for youtube**	keyword research **tips**
google keyword research	keyword research **process**
how to do keyword research	keyword research **methodology**

Step 5: Check for Head Terms and Long-Tail Keywords

Head terms are usually shorter and more generic, and long-tail keywords are longer keyword phrases containing three or more words. The next step is to ensure that you have a mix of both long-tail terms and head terms as it will provide you a keyword strategy that is well-adjusted for short-term and long-term goals.

Those head terms are popular search terms with high amounts of search volume. This means that the competition will be steep to rank for that keyword or phrase, both organically and paid advertising. For businesses just starting out or those that are smaller and/or working with a limited budget, targeting long-tail keywords can help you rank higher, faster without having to spend ridiculous amounts of money to get there.

Consider this. If we were to search for the term "wealth manager" we're likely to see some pretty big names in the coveted top results. If we were to convert that into a long tail keyword such as "wealth manager in Annapolis, MD" we see the competition is a bit more on par with that of a small to mid-sized business.

Indeed, there are a couple of creative approaches to achieving a top spot on the search engines and driving more traffic to your website organically, outside of targeting those harder keywords. As a business, you're providing a solution to a problem. As a wealth manager, some of the things you may do is retirement planning, create a custom financial plan, investment strategies, etc. Tailoring some of your keywords around specifically what you do versus your industry as a whole can be really valuable.

Some of those keywords may in fact be a question in itself. Have you ever queried the search engines with a specific question? You're not alone. We queried for "what is a long tail keyword" and in the image below you can see the answer to our question is found in a *featured snippet*, but also there are more results in the "people also search for". Take a look.

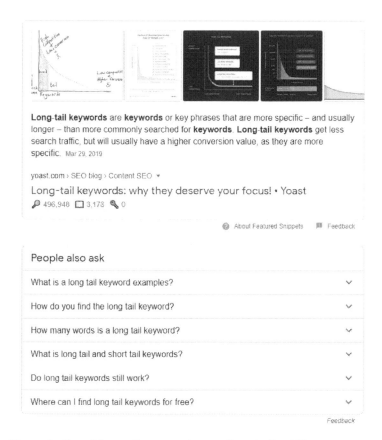

Long-tail keywords are keywords or key phrases that are more specific – and usually longer – than more commonly searched for keywords. Long-tail keywords get less search traffic, but will usually have a higher conversion value, as they are more specific. Mar 29, 2019

yoast.com › SEO blog › Content SEO ▾

Long-tail keywords: why they deserve your focus! • Yoast
🔍 496,948 ▢ 3,178 🔖 0

⦿ About Featured Snippets   ▥ Feedback

People also ask

What is a long tail keyword examples?	∨
How do you find the long tail keyword?	∨
How many words is a long tail keyword?	∨
What is long tail and short tail keywords?	∨
Do long tail keywords still work?	∨
Where can I find long tail keywords for free?	∨

Feedback

Step 6: See How Competitors Rank for These Terms

Just because a keyword or keyword phrase is essential to your competitor, does not mean it must be vital for you. Nevertheless, knowing which keywords your competitor is trying to rank for is an excellent way to reevaluate your list of words.

If the competitor is ranking for a particular keyword that is present on your list, it makes sense to improve your ranking for those terms and think about the avoided terms as an excellent opportunity to own market share on essential terms.

When conducting competitor research, it's important to have a clear understanding of who your competitors are. This doesn't necessarily mean the exact company names of all your competitors, but rather a big corporation isn't going to be a competitor of a small business, even if they are in the same industry. The fact is they have a much larger budget than a small business and likely have access to resources that a small business may not. When determining who your direct competitors are, some things you'll want to consider is this:

- Traffic to website
- Size of business (the bigger the business, the higher the budget)
- Locale (if your business is local and not national)

There are several tools out there that can help you determine what keywords your competitor is ranking for such as Moz, SEMrush and SpyFu to name a few. You're not doing anything shady by checking out the competition. In fact, your competitors are likely doing the same exact thing.

You could even work backwards if there's perhaps a keyword or phrase you're looking to rank for. Try querying the search engines for that keyword to see who ranks in the top spots for it and conduct your competitor research on those companies. If you're looking at competitors who are outside of your budget (i.e. larger companies/corporations), it's safe to say you may not see a high Return on Investment or be able to rank high for those keywords with a limited budget.

Step 7: Use Google AdWords Keyword Planner to Crop Keyword List

Once you have attained the right mix of keywords, the next step is to narrow down the list with more quantitative data. There are several tools available for this task, but Google AdWords Keyword Planner is an excellent choice for starting up. In order to get to Google's Keyword Planner, you'll need to sign up for a Google AdWords account. You do not need to pay for any advertisements to use the keyword planner.

Use any tool of your preference to highlight any words on your list with very high or low search volume. Use terms that provide you with the best balance to achieve your goals. Remember that the goal is to find keywords that you'll actually have a chance at ranking for and that your potential customers are actually using to query the search engines for. You're looking for the monthly search volume (i.e. how many people are searching for that keyword) and the metric showing how difficult it is to rank for that keyword or phrase.

Using Keywords to Rank Higher

You've got your list of keywords. Now what? Now it's time to generate some content and get those keywords on your website. You want to make sure that your main web copy (main pages and subpages such as the homepage, about, services, etc.) have the appropriate keywords interspersed throughout your content. You want to use no more than one to two keywords or phrases per page and each term should be on the page you're trying to rank for that keyword at least three times. This signals to the search engines that the keywords are important.

However, be careful not to over optimize as it could make your website show as spam to the search engines, which could downrank your website.

Another item Google and the other search engines will take into account is if the keywords appear naturally. Google is all about providing an optimal user experience. So, if you're just randomly stuffing keywords in your page for the sake of having them on there, Google isn't going to place much value on that page and may in fact penalize you for it. Obviously, that is counterintuitive to reaching your goals so ensure your keywords fit into a sentence and paragraph naturally.

An example of *natural* keyword placement is this:

Dental emergencies can happen at any time, even during a pandemic. If you're experiencing a dental emergency during COVID-19, you'll want to call an <u>experienced emergency dentist</u> *to be seen right away.*

Can you spot our key phrase? If you guessed "experienced emergency dentist" you'd be right. See how the wording just fits in with the content? That's what is meant by the term *natural*.

Build an SEO Friendly FAQ Page

When combing through keywords and eyeing up the metrics, you are sure to come across whole questions that people are querying the search engines for. While those are great to use in a blog, you can also use those questions to build a killer FAQ (*Frequently Asked Question*) page on your site as an additional resource. This can help you 1) provide value as *people are* **_actually querying_** *the search* *engines* for that question and 2) hitting on some valuable keywords to help improve your search engine ranking.

Again, it takes more than one article or answer to really bump you up in rank, so following up on this question and expanding on the answer in your blog section can take you that much farther.

Complimenting Your Keyword Efforts

Something you'll want to keep in mind is that it can take 4 to 6 months before you really notice any improvements in rankings and that keywords alone are not enough to get you to the top spot. There are about 200 different factors that Google and their bots take into account when determining how your website and page should rank. One thing you'll want to work on in addition to your keywords is increasing your Domain Authority.

Domain Authority - a term created by Moz - predicts how well a website will rank. The score is calculated by a number of factors including backlinks and keywords to name a few. Some people take the DA score as the end all, be all. While it is a very useful tool, it is really meant to be used as a guideline, an approximation if you will. The ideal DA range varies by industry, so don't get too hung up on the score. Newer websites and those who have rebranded may find they have a low DA, this is normal. Websites that have been around for a little while, have quality links back to their website and are ranking for some keywords should be looking for a score upwards of at least 15.

Moz has a great (and free) tool that you can use to learn more about your website's DA and that of your competitors. There are actually several free tools that they offer in addition to their paid offerings. The link explorer tool is the one you'll want to use to check out DA. This will also show you your backlinks, inbound links and ranking keywords.

Keyword Planning for Success

Armed with knowledge and a list of tools, you can now go forth and conquer your content. I know it's been mentioned a few times already, but if you're really looking to boost your search engine ranking, you'll need to spend time on other aspects of SEO. And remember, it can take *at least* four to six months before you start noticing any ranking improvements.

Understanding User Intent

When it comes to SEO, you really need to take into account *user intent.* When they query the search engines for specific topics, are they pursuing or are they ready to make a purchase? Does your product, service or article have words in it that could mean something different? People like to get creative - and that is GREAT! However, if we name our product after a famous landmark, it will not only make it more difficult for us to rank for that keyword, but also we may be attractive users who are not looking for that product or service, but rather more information on the landmark.

In order to identify the user's intent, you have to put yourself in the shoes of your customer. Often, we are too focused on just selling that we don't actually think about what the customer may want or need.

This chapter may leave you feeling like you've just had an English lesson, but nevertheless, I have faith that you'll be able to survive!

Take a look at the SEO keywords and phrases that you've identified. Now, break those keywords and phrases down into nouns, verbs, meaning, relationship, etc. Are there synonyms to the words used that could *also* be used to find you?

Are the keywords using prefixes and/or suffixes?

Understanding the elements behind the keywords you're targeting can help you better understand the user intent.

Now, let's add in an element of *intent modifiers*…

What the what is that? Intent modifiers take phrases like "personalized Christmas ornaments" to a phrase like "personalized Christmas ornaments near me" or "best personalized Christmas ornaments".

This gives our phrase a higher intent, meaning our users are expressing a higher shopping intent. They are on the hunt.

If you're ready to interject some higher intent keywords in your SEO strategy, have a look at this website:

https://www.adamriemer.me/50-modifiers-boost-seo-drive-sales/

They provide a list of generic intent modifiers that could be used to ramp up your efforts.

A Simple Guide to Heading Tags and How to Use Them Effectively

Today in this guide, we will be discussing a subtle and small SEO hack that can significantly improve the performance of your website or blog post content. We are referring to *Heading Tags (H-Tags)*.

Some people might be more acquainted with these than others, particularly those who are in the marketing industry, developers or software engineers. We are sure that many of you even use them while preparing content for your webpages, regardless of realizing their SEO value or not. However, for everyone else who is left wondering just what a Heading Tag is and why it's so important, we'll take a closer look at it as we go along.

We use heading tags in everything we publish online, including this blog post that you are reading right now. In fact, you will witness more of them as you continue down the post, so try to spot them. Follow this guide to learn what are heading tags and how to use them to improve your content effectively.

What Are Heading Tags?

Before we move further, let's make sure that we are all on the same page. Up until now, we have used two heading tags in the guide:

• H1 for the main title at the top of the page (*A Simple*

Guide to Heading Tags and How to Use Them Effectively)
- H2 for this subsection (*What Are Heading Tags?*)

And as we move further down the guide, there will be several more used as well, so be on the lookout!

By definition, heading tags are HTML (hypertext markup language) tags that denote headers on a blog post or website. To make it even simpler to understand, tags are codes that inform a web browser how the website or blog content should be displayed on the page. They're particularly valuable in that they help the search engines, like Google, index your website. If your Heading Tags aren't used appropriately, the search engines may get confused and downrank your website as a result.

How to Use Heading Tags Effectively?

There are six kinds of heading tags i.e., from H1 to H6. Each tag is ranked from highest to lowest based on their significance and is distinctly illustrated by their font size.

H1 Tag

The H1 tag will normally be the title of the blog post or the web page, and although it is best practice to use one H1 tag per post, there should not be any <u>negative SEO impact</u> in case you decide to use them more than once. Marketers are probably cringing at that last statement. However, that information was taken directly from Google, the search engine god that they are. Please note again that using H1 only once per page is *strongly encouraged*.

Ensure that you include primary keywords that you're trying to rank for in this tag to allow search engines to understand what keywords you want the page/content to rank for.

H2 Tag

H2 tags are generally used as primary subheadings and considered to be trivial on-page ranking factors. Therefore, we advise using them to incorporate a few synonyms of your primary keyword whenever appropriate.

This makes sense when Google analyzes a post or page heading to understand what it is about, hence including keywords in the H2 tags can allow search engines to comprehend that the content is about those keywords. Again, if the search engines can't figure out the context of the page, they won't be able to index the page appropriately and may downrank it as a result. Do not try to over optimize your webpage with H2 tags for the sake of optimizing.

H3 to H6 Tags

The remaining tags followed by the H2 tag must be used to represent the rest of the sub-heading hierarchy within a specific page or blog post.

The most crucial thing is that each heading or subheading must clearly define the content section it begins and logically structures the page or post.

 Here is an excellent example of a logically structured post may look like:

- H1: What is market gardening farming?
  - H2: The benefits of market gardening farming

- H3: Higher profits
- H3: Experimentation
- H3: Less labor

- H2: The shortcomings of market gardening farming

  - H3: Limited produce
  - H3: Requires diligence

Pro Tip: Always structure your headings well and use primary keywords in them.

When to Use Heading Tags?

Whether you are working on a blog post or website pages, make sure to include heading tags on each page! Using them effectively will provide a hierarchical structure to your content and help readers navigate the post quickly.

It is vital to ensure that structure is not disrupted, and tags are not missed out. Failure to do so will confuse Google and make the content unstructured. Generally, H1-H4 tags are used majorly for webpages and blog posts, whereas H5 and H6 are used for very long and in-depth pieces of writing.

Why Use Headings Tags?

There are a number of reasons why your website and all of the content on it should use heading tags, including:

1. Boost SEO

2. Improve Accessibility

3. Provide Structure

Boost SEO

While Heading Tags may not directly impact your SEO, it can indirectly impact it in a number of ways when employed correctly and effectively. It creates content of a higher quality that is easier to read and a better text is favorable for users, and thus better for your SEO. The search engines prefer content that they are able to understand and classify but also, they prefer content that provides optimal user experiences.

If visitors do not easily find what they are looking for, they may leave your webpage and turn to your competition's website to answer their queries. This is why the structure and headings used in your content would impact your SEO.

Improve Accessibility

Heading structure is vital for accessibility, especially for visitors who cannot easily read via a screen. As heading tags are in HTML, a person reading from a screen can easily view and understand the article structure and content.

By listening or reading the headings on a post, visually challenged people can decide whether they want to read more about the content or not. Moreover, screen readers provide shortcuts to jump from one heading to another to provide navigation to readers.

And let's not forget that what's good for accessibility is also favorable for SEO!

Provide Structure

Heading tags allow readers to navigate through your blog post or website effortlessly, providing an optimal user experience. Therefore, it is vital to indicate what a paragraph or section is about, or visitors (and search engine bots) would not know what to expect.

Readers generally like to quickly skim through content, to decide which section of the content they are going to read. Adding h-tags drastically helps them do that as the skimming process becomes significantly more accessible for readers when it contains headings.

All About That Meta, Yo

Other key elements to nailing your on-site SEO are your meta data tags. Fair warning, this section may be a little more technical than others, but we'll try to keep it on a level that even beginners can understand, because after all, that's who this book is written for!

Every web page encompasses meta tags, but they are only visible in the HTML code.

Now, you need to understand that some tags are essential for SEO, while others have little to no impact on rankings.

But first, let's answer the question, *"what are meta tags?"*

What Are Meta Tags?

Meta tags offer information about a webpage in the HTML of a document. This data is known as *"metadata"* and though it›s not exhibited on the page itself, it can be read by web crawlers and search engines.

Search engines like Google use metadata from meta tags to comprehend additional info about a webpage. They can use this data to display snippets in search results for ranking purposes, and occasionally they can even ignore meta tags.

Example of meta tags encompass the **<title>** and **<description>** elements.

Why Do Meta Tags Matter?

As mentioned earlier, meta tags provide more information

about your website to search engines like Google and visitors who encounter your website in the SERP. Meta tags can be optimized to highlight the most crucial elements of your content and help your site to stand out in search results.

In addition, search engines are increasingly valuing a good user experience, which involves making sure that your website gratifies a visitor's query in the best possible way. Meta tags can help you achieve this by ensuring that searchers can view upfront what your web page is about in a useful and concise manner.

Some types of meta tags deal with page structure and make sure that your website is easy to navigate, whereas there are others that tell search engines which portions of your page are vital and which to oversee. Utilizing the right meta tags in the best possible way is all about communicating to search engines the following:

- What your web page is about
- How to read it
- Who should see it

There are several different types of meta tags that satisfy different roles, but keep in mind that not all of them are relevant to search engine optimization (SEO). However, we have picked out the six most vital meta tags for SEO that you must use and to know about in this quick guide.

6 Essential Types of Meta Tags for SEO

#1: Title Tags

The title tag is your prime and most vital anchor. The <title>

component generally appears as a clickable headline in the search engine results, and it also emerges up in browsers and on social networks. Title tags are positioned in the <head> of your page and are used to deliver a comprehensive and clear idea of what the webpage is all about.

But do they really have any significant impact on rankings?

Over the past few years, user behavior factors have been considerably deliberated as logical proof of relevance and a ranking signal. Even Google representatives acknowledge the impact of title tags here and there.

There's no doubt that the webpage's title is still the first thing a searcher sees in SERPs and decides if the webpage is likely to answer their search intent. Therefore, a well-written title tag can enhance the number of traffic and clicks - which has at least some impact on your rankings.

What search engines like Google are looking at is the *'entire picture,'* and they tend to assess a webpage›s content as a whole, but remember, the cover of a book always matters first– particularly when it comes to interaction with searchers.

Best practices for title tags

- Give every webpage a unique title that defines the page's content accurately and concisely.
- Keep the titles only up to fifty-sixty characters long as long titles are reduced to around 600-700px on search engine results.
- Try to put primary keywords first but logically and naturally.

#2: Meta Description Tags

Meta description tags also dwell in the <head> of a page and are generally (though certainly not always) demonstrated in a SERP snippet along with a page URL and title.

Remember, meta description tags itself are not a ranking factor. But for anyone trying to amplify their click-throughs and enhance their brand SERPs, it is indeed a unique opportunity. Here are a few things you ought to know:

The meta description captures the largest part of a search engine result snippet and entices searchers to click on your website by promising a comprehensive and clear solution to their query.

1. It impacts the number of clicks you receive and might also decrease bounce rates and improve CTR if the pages' content fulfills the promises. That is why the meta description should be realistic, inviting, and distinctly reflect the content of your webpage.

2. If your meta description encompasses the keywords a searcher used in their query, they'll appear on the search engine results in **bold**. This will greatly help you to stand out and inform the searcher what they will find on your page.

A decent way to figure out what to write in your description, or what works best for your specific topic right now is to conduct some competition research. See how your top-ranking competitors fill out their own meta descriptions to get an idea about the best use cases.

Best practices for meta description tags

- Give every webpage a unique description that clearly and concisely reflects the value the page carries.
- Google's description snippets usually max out around 150 to 160 characters (involving spaces).
- Incorporate your most important keywords, so they can get highlighted on the actual search engine results but be watchful to avoid keyword stuffing. You should not make your meta description tag merely a combination of keywords you are targeting.

#3: Heading Tags – H1 to H6

- Heading tags are HTML tags used to classify headings and subheadings within your page content from other forms of text, for example, paragraph text.

While H2-H6 tags are viewed not as vital to search engines, but the proper usage of the H1 tag has been accentuated in several industry studies.

But at the same time, many marketers keep telling us that heading tags are not ranking factors at all, and certainly not in the sense of 'hierarchy'- meaning, the H1 tag isn't more significant than H2; which isn't more vital than H3, and so on.

Instead, what you should be thinking about is that heading tags are essential for content and text organization, and hence they should be taken seriously. Using heading tags can indeed add up to the architecture of your webpage's content.

- **For users:** heading tags are like guiding beacons in a wall of text, navigating them through the webpage

content and making it easier to understand.
- **For search engines**: it is easier to understand and read the well-organized page content than to crawl through structural problems.

Both these factors augment the significance of careful optimization, where trivial details add up to the big, user-friendly and SEO picture and thus leads to improved rankings.

Best practices for heading tags
- Keep your heading tags relevant to the portion of text they're defining. Just because they are not a ranking factor does not mean search engines do not take them into consideration.
- Always have your heading tags reflect the sentiments of the content they're placed over. Try to avoid headings like "Chapter 1, Chapter 2, Chapter 3…".
- Do not overuse the heading tags and the keywords in them. Always make them readable for users.

#4: Image Alt Attributes
The image alt attribute is included in an image tag to define its contents. Alt attributes are essential in terms of on-site optimization for two main reasons:

1. Alt-text is presented to visitors if any individual image can't be loaded or if the pictures are disabled.

2. Alt attributes deliver context because search engines cannot "see" images.

According to Google, assisting search engines to understand what the pictures are about and how they related to the rest of the content might help them serve a webpage for suitable search queries.

A well-thought image alt description is also vital if you'd like to rank in Google Images. Though, remember the significance of relevancy: it is not just that the titles, alt text, and captions ought to be relevant to the picture, but the picture itself should be positioned in its appropriate, relevant context.

Best practices for image alt attributes

- Do your best to augment the most prominent images, such as product images, training images, or infographics – images that are most likely to look up in search engines.
- Add image alt text on webpages where there is not a lot of content apart from the images.
- Keep the image alt text descriptive and clear enough, utilize your keywords reasonably, and ensure they fit naturally into the whole canvas of the webpage's content.

#5: Robots Meta Tag

A web page-level robots meta tag alongside content= *"noindex"* element commands the search engines not to index any specific page.

A *"nofollow"* attribute orders not to follow any links on that webpage.

Although these tags do not directly correlate with rankings, in several cases, they might have some influence on how your website looks overall in the eyes of search engines. For example, Google highly disregards thin content.

You might not produce it intentionally, but there are some

pages that happen to have little value for users but are yet necessary to have on the website for various reasons.

You may also have placeholder or *"draft"* webpages that you must publish while they›re not yet completed or optimized to their best. Therefore, you most probably would not want such pages to be taken into consideration the overall quality of your site if being evaluated.

In many other cases, you might want certain webpages to stay out of search engine results as they feature some form of special deal that's supposed to be accessible through a direct link only, for example, from a newsletter.

Lastly, if you own a sitewide search option, Google suggests you close custom results pages that can be crawled indeterminately and waste bot's resources on no special content.

In the above cases, nofollow and noindex tags are of great importance, as they provide you certain control over your website while it is viewed by the search engines.

Best practices for robots meta tag
- Close unfinished/ unnecessary webpages with thin content that have trivial value and no intent to emerge in the SERPs.
- Close webpages that unjustly waste crawl budget.
- Make sure you do not mistakenly restrict essential pages from indexing.

#6: Viewport Meta Tag

A viewport meta tag helps you to configure how your pages would be scaled and shown on any device. Generally, the viewport tag and the value will look as follows:

```
<meta name="viewport" content="width=device-
width, initial-scale=1"/>
```

Where **'width=device-width'** would make the webpage match the display›s width in device-independent pixels, and ‹**initial scale=1'** would create a 1:1 relationship between device-independent pixels and CSS pixels, taking screen orientation into consideration.

This meta tag is a no-brainer to add, particularly in times like these, when users search the web with multiple devices such as mobile phones, tablets, laptops, etc.

Now, the viewport meta tag has nothing directly to do with searching engine rankings, but it has a ton to do with the user experience. It is particularly crucial to consider the variety of devices that are being utilized nowadays and the prominent shift to mobile browsing.

As with several of the tweaks and tags we have discussed in this guide, looking after the viewport meta tag will definitely be something your users appreciate. On the other hand, if you neglect it, your bounce rates and CTR could suffer.

Meta tags for SEO certainly play a key role in search engine rankings, but it is important to understand that not all meta tags can help you. In our experience, if you wish to rank high on Google, then you must also focus on user satisfaction and high-quality content.

Image Optimization

Whether you are an online content developer, blogger, or writer producing articles for a newspaper or an online magazine, odds are you'll find yourself questioning if your content needs an image or not…

The answer is always: **Yes!**

Images not only bring life to your article, but they also contribute to your site's SEO. This article will briefly touch upon '**Image Optimization'** and some foolproof image SEO tips.

Why is it important to use images in articles?

When used correctly, images can help readers to understand your article better. The longstanding saying – *"A picture is worth a thousand words"* doesn't probably apply to Google, but it is indeed true when you have to spice up a myriad of dull words.

It's recommended to include images in every blog/article you produce to make them more interesting in a nutshell. Moreover, as visual search is increasingly gaining popularity, it can provide you with a nice boost in traffic.

Some Tips for Image Optimization

Use these image SEO tips to maximize the findability and speed of your articles.

#1: Choose the correct format

Cracking all the numerous image formats can feel like the first time placing an order at Taco Bell. But before you start adding pictures to your website, ensure you have picked the best file type. Though there are several image formats to choose from, JPEG and PNG are the most commonly used for the web.

JPEG: You might lose image quality; however, you can tweak it to find a decent balance.

PNG: Gives better quality images but has a larger file size.

Tip #2: Compress your image file size

As per HTTP Archive, 21 percent of a total web page's weight is due to images, affecting your website's loading speed. The bigger the image file size, the slower it loads and vice versa. That is why we highly recommend you compress your images before uploading them on your website. To do this, you can use apps like Adobe Photoshop, TinyPNG, etc.

Tip#3: Create unique images

If you fill your site with stock imagery, it will be challenging for you to stand out among the crowd due to unoriginality as a plethora of other websites are using the same stock of photos.

Although you might have your stock images impeccably optimized, know that it will not have the same impact or offer potential SEO benefits as a high-quality, original image. The more original your images are, the better experience for the visitor, and the improved your odds are of ranking on relevant searches.

Some other key tips for image optimization are:

Ensure the alternative and image text are relevant to the page.

- Ensure your on-site SEO elements - metadata, structured data, etc.- pair with your visuals.
- Develop an image sitemap for crawlability, or ensure your images are featured in the sitemap.

You must understand that optimizing images for search engines is no joke. With increasing progress in voice search technology, media is gaining importance, and your whole website will benefit from the image SEO tips discussed above.

Let's dive a bit deeper into the how…

Image SEO: Alt-Text

What the heck is alt-text and does image SEO *really* matter? If you're one of the ones asking that, well, you're in the right place. The short version is that *yes* image SEO matters.

If you were to query Google for something and hop over to the image results, what would you see?

If you've optimized your images effectively, you'll be able to *organically* rank well in Google's Image Search - yet another place to reach potential clients.

In the example above, we've queried "legal marketing agency" and you can see two images from Precision Legal Marketing. That's because our image SEO is on point (insert winky face).

But the value in image SEO and alt-text doesn't stop with simply ranking well (though isn't that a good enough reason to just do it??).

What is Alt-Text

Alt-Text is the written copy/text that appears if your image fails to load on a user's screen. It also benefits those users needing to use screen-reading tools to describe images to them - such as visually impaired readers. Not only that, but it also helps search engines crawl and rank your website.

Mind blown; I know.

Alt-Text is also known as "alt attributes", "alt descriptions", and occasionally (though wrongly so) "alt tags". While many CMS (Content Management System) - such as WordPress, for instance - have made it easy to quickly input alt-text without writing code, alt-text is typically written like this:

```
<img src="steveshappydance.gif" alt="Steve's
Happy Dance">
```

The key to your alt-text is to be descriptive; Explain what exactly in the image. Is it a picture of a "dog" *or* a picture of a "dog running in the park playing fetch"? Obviously, the second choice there is the optimal one.

Avoid leaving the alt-text of an image blank. Also, you'll want to avoid keyword stuffing in your alt-text as if the hounds of hell were on your heels. Keyword stuffing is where you jam loads of keywords into the alt-text of an image to try to rank for *all* of those keywords, even if the keywords are not relevant to the image. Going back to our dog running in the park playing fetch example....

"Dog, dog park, dog sitting services, kennels, dog boarding"

You should **_not_** do that. Why? Google can tell what you're doing and may ding you for it. Avoid the possibility of penalties by doing the right thing. You'll thank me for that later.

Alt-Text Best Practices

Looking to go out there and optimize your images with your newfound knowledge? Here are some best practices to help you optimize your images.

- Be descriptive and keep it in line with the image's subject and context.
- Try to stay around 125 characters or less.
- Do not start your alt-text by saying "picture of" - they know it's a picture and you're wasting characters.
- Use keywords sparingly - don't overoptimize or keyword stuff.
- Each image should have a different alt-text as the images are usually not the exact same.

SEO Value of Internal Linking

Nearly every article you come across on the internet regarding internal linking starts with a discussion of how complex yet important the subject matter is.

On the one hand, internal linking is an extremely simple concept, and everybody should be doing it.

- While on the other, the process, theory, and best practices of internal linking can get excessively complex.
- It is both simple and advanced. But irrespective of how basic or complex you think it's; no one will argue about this: *It is important!*

In this article, we want to deliver knowledge related to the SEO value of internal linking that can benefit both experienced and amateurs' SEOs.

What Is Internal Linking?

An internal link joins one page of a website to another page of the same website. The target and source domains are the same in an internal link.

What Is the Purpose of Internal Linking?

Internal linking has three major purposes:

1. It aids in website navigation.
2. Defines the hierarchy and architecture of a website.

3. Distributes ranking power and page authority throughout the website.

The Concept Behind Internal Linking

The primary concept of internal linking is that it strengthens and bolsters the overall search-optimized value of a site. It does so by offering prolonged sessions for users, clear paths for spiders, and a tight-knit network of posts and pages.

But how do you do it? Below are some foolproof ways to effectively use internal linking.

6 Foolproof Ways to Effectively Use Internal Linking

#1: Produce a myriad of content

To generate lots of internal links, you need to have many internal pages. The first step towards producing a killer internal linking strategy is to design a killer content marketing strategy. Remember, you cannot have one without the other.

When you generate a plethora of content, you will acquire a lot of linkable content. The more links you attach to more places, the superior your internal linking strategy will be.

#2. Use anchor text

Your internal links must use anchor text than linked images. Keep in mind that image links work fine, but provided that images aren't the chief source of links, and supposing the image is appropriately alt-tagged.

In addition, the correct use of anchor text opens the door to new horizons. Evidently, you do not want optimized anchors. Therefore, just use unoptimized, natural sentence fragments as anchor text, and you will be just fine.

No overthinking it. No cute tricks. Just highlight it, link it, and be done!

*Refer to our chapter on anchor text for a more in depth understanding of what it is, and how to use it effectively.

#3: Link deep

Remember, the deeper your links go, the more fruitful it is for your internal link strategy. There are two kinds of links you must avoid using in your content:

Contact us: This is a very common mistake of several who're starting out in content marketing. As a share of their obligatory 'call to action' at the end of an article or blog post, they might come up with something like:

"Reach out to us by giving us a call and learn more about our amazing services!"

Then, they link the content to the "contact us" utilizing the anchor "give us a call." But never link to the contact us page till it's absolutely necessary.

Homepage: Many websites have linked way too many internal links to their homepage. You should rather fortify internal pages to boost the overall SEO of your website than merely point more links to your homepage.

The best internal links and the most natural links in content marketing strategy are deeply rooted within the structure of a website.

#4: Utilize links that are natural for the user

Internal linking demands a user-focused approach to add value and information. The link value that gets disseminated throughout the website is secondary to this key point — *delivering value to the reader.*

One of the upshot benefits of internal linking is that it enhances user engagement on your website. When a visitor sees an informative and valuable link that truly counters the context of the content, they're more likely to click on that link.

Now, it can be an external link; remember, as long as it is delivering something that the users want to read or are interested in, it's worth linking. Similarly, if that link is internal, the website visitor will stay longer on your page and become more involved in your site experience.

#5: Use relevant links

Internal linking, as we have made clear, is less scientific and rigorous than some people might think. Nonetheless, you still have to be intentional! Do not just link for the sake of linking, instead link to the content that's *relevant* to the source context.

#6: Use follow links

Follow links are an excellent way to build the internal link architecture of your content marketing.

In the past, one internal linking strategy was to 'nofollow' most of the links on a webpage to intensify the link juice to a particular page. Despite the confusion and uproar in the wake of the 'nofollow' link, most marketers now agree that it is a good approach.

Many believe that nofollow links can allow websites to avoid problems with search engines - believing they're selling influence or involved in schemes considered as unacceptable SEO practices.

However, utilizing nofollow links isn't a strategy you use as part of your internal content links. The link usefulness should flow freely to and from internal pages, instead of getting stopped up by a nofollow.

Keep in mind that content links are a strong signal to both the user and the search engine that the content you are linking to is relevant, informative, and useful. And this is something that all readers want. Therefore, never forget that internal linking is primarily a tool to help the reader, and in doing so, you are also helping your SEO.

The SEO Value of Blogs

You've conducted keyword research and are ready to get rocking, but what do you do with it outside of optimizing your pages (copy, title tags, meta, etc.)? Just including a keyword on your main page isn't enough to get your site to the coveted first page result in most cases, which means you'll need to keep building on those keywords to continue to push higher in the rankings. How do you do that? One of the biggest ways to do this is through blogging, which is the first step in our journey through content.

All About Blogging

There are those that may prefer the stance of "it's not a competition". If you'd prefer to think of it another way, think of it like this. Creating content without optimizing means you MAY be able to rank on the search engines, but it's not likely to be very high - meaning you're the 47th result to show up for a specific keyword/keyphrase. That means that you're not on the first page, not even on page two or three of the search results. Let's look at some statistics:

According to HubSpot, there are 34,000 Google queries PER SECOND and over one trillion searches per month. That's a LOT of searches! Of those searches, 75 percent of users never go past the first page. What does this mean? That means that unless you're ranking on the first page for what your customers are looking for, you're not very visible. With all of that in mind, let's jump in.

Benefits of Blogging

We talked about a couple of the benefits of blogging briefly already, but let's dive a bit deeper into the sea of benefit.

- Thought leader
- Relevant, value-driven content
- Drive traffic to your website
- Keywords/Search engine ranking
- Continuously updated content

Many business owners either don't have time or don't see the value in blogging and so often, don't take advantage.

Thought Leader

What is a thought leader?

A thought leader can be an individual or a company that is regarded by prospects, clients, associates and even competitors as a trusted source or authority within their respective industry. A thought leader offers unique advice, guidance and provides inspiration to others in their industry.

How do you become a thought leader?

If you're wondering how to become a thought leader in your industry, you're not alone. Establishing yourself as a thought leader takes time and effort. You also can't just declare yourself a thought leader - the elusive title is one that is bestowed upon you. Continue to produce relevant and value-driven content and it will come.

There is value in the early stages as well. You may not be an influencer or even well-known within your industry, but that doesn't mean that the content you're producing is worthless. Your clients and potential clients want to know that you're an expert in your industry - or at least competent enough that they can rely on your product or services. Which brings us to our next benefit.

Relevant, Value-Driven Content

It can take years to establish yourself as an expert to those in your industry. It may take less time to prove yourself to your clients. Producing relevant, value-driven content for free can help your clients and potential clients come to trust you. It can help to instill trust in those who are likely to frequent your business.

Understand your client's problem and provide the solution. Build a relationship with them built on trust for a lasting and fruitful relationship.

Drive Traffic to Your Website

By producing relevant and value-driven content, such as blogs, you're providing a reason for people to visit your website AND to spend time there. Google Analytics is a beast and is also essential. If you haven't put a Google Analytics code on your website, you're behind the curve. That is a beast for another day, and we won't go into it in this book beyond telling you to install the code and talking about the bounce rate.

Some of the things you can monitor on Google Analytics is how much traffic your website is getting, when the busiest day and time of the week are, how many visits to each page and your bounce rate. Again, there is so much more that you could do, but we're not going to go into that in this book.

The bounce rate is the rate of visitors to your website who navigate away after viewing only one page. A higher bounce rate means that people aren't staying on your website and it may be a sign that you should consider restructuring your home page. If your website has a higher bounce rate, search engines like Google won't place much value in your website and it may cause you to rank lower.

Failure is the ladder to success.

If your bounce rate is high, it may be indicative that you need to change things or add in some valuable content, but it does not mean that you should quit. Failure paves the way to success; You just need to get up and try again. When we first started our company, our website was atrocious! However, after identifying the problem we sought the solution to improve our website and the overall experience for our users. So, just keep on keeping on. We have faith in you!

All right. Enough of that and back to the learning. How can blogging help your bounce rate? Well, by providing content on your website, such as blogs, that provides engaging information that your audience would actually *want* to read, it will keep them on your website longer and decrease the bounce rate. Do we need to say that last part again??

Engaging content, such as a blog, entices users to spend more time on your website and therefore will decrease the bounce rate. That lower bounce rate will signal to the search engines that you are producing engaging content and may improve your ranking for certain keywords. Which leads us to our next subtopic.

Keywords and Search Engine Ranking

When we broach the subject of keywords/keyphrases, the majority of business owners we've spoken to have no idea what we're talking about. Look at keywords from this standpoint:

You are a potential customer who is looking to find a new dentist. Perhaps you've asked a friend for a referral and then looked them up online to get their contact info and check out their reviews. Maybe you've just gone straight to the search engine. Either way, at some point we end up at the search engine. What do you do now? You type in a keyword or keyphrase to bring up results that are relevant to your query. For this example, let's say you typed in "family dentist in Orlando, FL". (I've got theme parks on the mind!)

If there are let's say 10,000 people searching for those exact keywords every single month and your website doesn't have them, you are not competing for customers. You're not even in the running. Not even in the bandstands. You will most likely _not_ be found by those 10k people who are looking for a family dentist in Orlando.

This is where we tell you that you need to do your homework. You need to find out what words and phrases your potential customers are querying and make sure they're on your website - and we don't mean one and done. While you should still conduct research on what people are querying, you should also check out what your competitors are doing. This can provide you a great jumping off point.

The trick is to make sure that they appear natural and that you aren't over optimizing your content in there.

Keyword stuffing can negatively impact your search engine ranking. There are loads of tools out there that can help you accomplish your keyword research - some free, most paid.

If you need a refresher on keyword research, hop back over to that chapter.

Continuously Updated Content

<u>Bottom Line Up Front (BLUF):</u> Websites who do not continually provide fresh content will be viewed as static websites (aka dead) by the search engines as you aren't offering up anything new.

The search engines use bots to crawl your website. The newer content your website provides, the more your website will be indexed. This does *not* mean that you will rank higher simply based on frequent indexing. It means that you'll have more *opportunities* to rank higher.

Google has over 200 factors that go into determining how well your website will rank in the search engines and it's all really a balancing act. Is your website credible? Does your content have the right blend of keywords? What is your website's authority? While you may feel like your answer to all of those is yes, what do the numbers tell you? How many keywords are you ranking for? How many quality backlinks does your website have? Are you producing relevant and engaging content to drive traffic?

Case Studies

The benefits of blogging are there, for sure, but not without a fair bit of effort. So, if you're going to make the effort, you'll probably want to know that it works before investing your time (and money if you're paying someone to do it for you) in blogging.

Steven Long, founder of Precision Legal Marketing, shared with us just how well blogging coupled with SEO worked during COVID-19 in the chapter on Leveraging Trending Topics:

> *"When COVID first hit we had a client in mid-town Manhattan literally go dark. Because courts were suddenly shuttered. With 8 attorneys on their staff, everyone had time to fill. So, we put them to work writing family law blog content related to COVID. We covered the gambit of what to do it your co-parent has COVID (do you still send your child to their house) to how to get along in quarantine with a spouse you know you want to divorce. Within days, we had 18-20 pieces published on the site. We have never posted new content for one client this quickly, so it was a real challenge for our team to maintain SEO integrity while essentially rushing this content. Within a week of publishing this content, we saw traffic literally double. We had national rank for COVID/divorce keywords and even out ranked major NYC news outlets and other national sites. While we don't want national traffic on the site per se, the traffic was mostly New Yorkers doing national broad keyword type searches. Google wasn't yet algorithmically caught up, so we immediately benefited. Months later, the sites traffic has stayed at those new levels, so it wasn't just a flash in the pan. The search engines were hungry for content, we fed them."*

10 Principles of Blogging

As with everything, there are some best practices, or principles, to blogging. Your heart may be in the right place with some well-meaning blogs, but when they're not optimized for users queries and the search engines, they may fall flat. And here's the best part? If you already have some blogs on your website, you can republish them as if they were new once you've updated them to be a bit more user and search engine friendly.

Let's take a look at the 10 principles of blogging.

1. *Define Your Target Audience* - Not everyone is your customer. Write to those who are likely to convert to clients. What common interests does your customer have? If you own a pet store, you know that your customers are all going to be interested in pets.

2. *Conduct Topic Research* - Seasons change, the economy goes through hardships, and every once in a while, a major event such as a pandemic occurs. Stay ahead of the curve by researching what topics are relent <u>at that time</u>. For instance, during COVID-19 many pet owners were concerned that their pets were either carriers or could contract the virus. Keeping your customers informed of these hot topics can drive traffic to your website and help build your brand awareness.

3. *Conduct Keyword Research* - We already talked about this one and why it's important. Have a look at what keywords you'd like your website to rank higher for and try to shape your blog around them. Going back to our pet shop example, we may want to rank higher for includes a selection of pet grooming

products. With more time being spent at home during the pandemic, pet owners were having to take grooming into their own hands. A blog on "Five Tips to Grooming Your Pet at Home" would be a topic that would elicit some interest and you could use the keywords for your grooming products in the article.

4. *Inbound and Outbound Links* - Inbound links are links in your article (or other section of your website) that link to other articles or sections of your website. Outbound links refer to links that go to other websites. As a general rule of thumb, you should have at least one or two of each in your article. Now, you're not just throwing a random URL in there, you're highlighting a word and then hyperlinking the word(s) to the inbound or outbound URL.

5. *SEO Formatting* - You can't escape SEO formatting! Just like the rest of your page, your blog or article should include a title, which will be your H1 tag (Heading Tag AKA H-Tag), and your subtitles which will be your H2, H3 and H4 tags. These tags are important as they help the search engine determine how to index your website. If the search engines get confused, you won't rank as high even if you've met all of the other factors in their algorithm.

6. *Minimum Word Count* - It's tempting to just throw a couple of paragraphs out there, but you should aim for a minimum of about 600 words. If you can, aim higher. While 600 words would have been enough to rank in prior years, these days you really need to have about 1500+ words to be competitive with those appearing on page one of the search engines.

7. *Ensure Readability* - Write to your reader. Many

businesses write as if they were writing to other professionals in the industry. What do I mean by that? Lawyers often have difficulty conveying a message that those of us without a background in law could really understand. That is often jokingly called "legalese". You've got to find a way of translating that legalese into a way that those without a background in your industry can understand. For instance, if someone is looking for a financial advisor to help create a financial plan and invest some money for retirement, they may not understand all of the terms like S&P 500, haircut (totally different meaning in financial talk!), bear market, etc. Before delving into a topic like that you must first clarify what a haircut is in financial speak.

When writing your blogs, you want to make sure that your readers can fully understand what you're putting out there. In addition to that, you want to put your best foot forward by ensuring your post is free of spelling and grammatical errors.

8. *Keep Opinions to Yourself & Avoid Controversial Topics* - It's tempting to join in those hot topics surrounding controversial issues, politics, or to express your opinion. Save that for your personal (and private) lives. Unless your business' brand is built around a certain controversial issue, you run the risk of alienating a percentage of your potential clients. Even worse, participating in a controversial issue may make your business go viral for all the wrong reasons, which could lead to you being forced to close shop.

9. *Be Objective* - Dial down the sales pitch. We've

all gotten called by some pushy salespeople who can't take no for an answer. Don't be that pushy salesperson. To really build your brand and a loyal following, provide them with relevant and valuable information less the sales pitch. It's okay to conclude your blog with a call to action, but you shouldn't be ramming your "buy now" pitch down their throats. You may offer an awesome product or service, but eventually your pushiness will be enough to drive them away.
Being objective also means being unbiased. Of course, you'll be biased towards your own products or services however, you should refrain from taking sides.

10. *Promote It!* - You just wrote a kick a$$ blog! Go out there and tell the world!! Share your blog on social media. Consider pushing your blogs out to Facebook, LinkedIn, Twitter, Instagram AND Google My Business. Not all of those will be relevant to all industries. Google My Business is a great way to put information out there, especially blogs, but is often underutilized for that purpose. It's free, your business should already have a GMB profile, so why not?! It's just one more way for you to drive traffic to your website.

Determining Whether Blogging is Working

Blogging is the long-haul game. There are no overnight success options and anyone who tells you otherwise is lying to you. Realistically, if your website's SEO is in good shape and you've optimized your website with the appropriate keywords and keyphrases, including your blog section, you're looking at about four to six months on average to start seeing results. Don't be discouraged. Keep working on your keywords and producing relevant, continuous content and your hard work will pay off.

Let's set some realistic expectations here as well. In four to six months when you start seeing results, you're most likely *not* going to be on page one. You may not even be hitting page two or three, but if you're in the top 50 you're going somewhere! When you start ranking for those keywords, keep building on them to continually improve your ranking. Remember that your competitors are still out there hustling. If you don't keep up with them or let your content grow stagnant, you'll lose any ground you've gained.

Here are some metrics you can use to measure some of the items we've talked about in this chapter.

To track the bounce rate (and various other metrics) on your website, you'll want to install a Google Analytics code on your website. You can download the app and track everything real-time on your phone. This tool is completely free.

Domain Authority (DA) is a ranking metric created by a software company called Moz. Moz has some really great - a couple free - tools on their website. One of those free tools is the link explorer. This tool will show you your DA and some of the factors that it took into account to give you that ranking. It will show you how your DA has changed over time, every link that links back to your website (backlinks), how many inbound links you have, how many and what keywords your website is ranking for, etc.

In addition to Moz, there are several other tools out there that you can use to track how you're ranking for keywords - most of them are paid. One of our favorite's is Rank Ranger. This tool offers quite a number of capabilities, including the ability to track keyword rank AND to conduct keyword research.

While you're checking out your own link in Moz, check out your competitor's website as well to give you some idea of links you could try to get a backlink from or even keywords you should be trying to rank for.

Can you tell I have a love for writing?! All right. This was a really long chapter, and we'll give you a break before diving into the next segment.

Bonus: FAQ Page

Another way you can continue to build on your keywords and the work you're committing to with blogging is to compliment those efforts with a Frequently Asked Question page on your website. When people query the search engines, they're querying specific keyphrases, and sometimes, even whole questions. Use those to your advantage to build a stellar FAQ page to provide value AND to hit on those keywords/phrases to give your SEO an extra boost.

Check out this link for an optimized FAQ page:

https://www.egaprocessserving.com/faq/

All of those questions use keywords and exact questions that people were querying the search engines for. Just like blogs, when possible, you want to make sure that you've reiterated the keyword/phrase/exact question in the body of the text to make sure the keywords signal their importance to the search engines. It bears repeating that they should also appear *naturally* and not just be randomly stuffed in there.

Infographics

Surely nobody wants to spend a lot of time reading and trying to comprehend pages of intricate facts and figures. It is unquestionably not a coincidence that so much of the information that we share and see online today is in some form of pictorial representation.

There is a myriad of information surrounding us that is possibly not easy to grasp or remember in the limited amount of time that we have. However, using infographics is certainly an effective way to convey complex data and figures to readers and helps them to effectively understand and absorb information promptly.

But what are infographics?

Here we've brought you a complete guide to infographics to help you understand everything about this effective information displaying tool.

What Are Infographics?

Simply put, infographics are pictorial representations of information, knowledge, or data, specially designed to exhibit complex information clearly and quickly. Moreover, they're great for improving cognition by utilizing graphics to augment the human visual system's ability to see trends and patterns.

Infographics are all about telling a story; they help readers organize data and make complex information visually digestible so that way, readers can easily and quickly process the information. Infographics are used for numerous reasons; they are concise, entertaining, eye-catching, and useful.

Infographic Components

Infographics comprise of the following elements:
- **Content Elements:** include statistics, references, and time frames.
- **Visual Elements:** involve color, reference icons, and graphics.
- **Knowledge Elements:** involves facts and figures.

Why are Infographics Used?
Usually, infographics are used for a few of the following reasons:

Create Awareness
Create brand visibility and awareness or spread the word about a vital cause.

Illustrate Data
Present facts, statistics, and figures visually using graphs, charts, and other graphic tools.

Summarize Lengthy Content
Encapsulate lengthy blog posts, reports, and videos into a bite-sized visual representation.

Draw a Comparison
Visually compare two or more services, products,

concepts, features, or brands.

Simplify Complex Information

Describe complex concepts with the help of visual illustrations and cues.

How Infographics Benefit Businesses

Infographics are very beneficial for businesses, and it greatly helps to pass on essential information to target audiences in a fun and easy way. The following are a few of the many benefits of infographics received by businesses.

1. Attractive and Engaging

   Infographics are more engaging, and fun as compared to plain text as they generally combine colors, images, content, and movement that naturally catches the eye. Valuable and relevant content is frequently reposted across the internet as well, leading to naturally occurring backlinks to your content.

2. Easy to View and Scan

   Most people forget a lot of what they have read and tend to have short space attention spans, but they do remember what they've seen.

3. Increased Traffic

   Infographics are greatly sharable for use around the web. For instance, an infographic published in a WordPress blog or website usually issues an embed code. The code generates an automatic link from the original site to yours.

4. Boost Brand Awareness

   Infographics can be used to reinforce a brand, simply because they are visually appealing. Creating an infographic embedded with your logo and with your brand prominently displayed is a powerful means of increasing brand awareness.

5. Search Engine Optimization

   The viral nature of infographics makes people link to your site. Infographics can easily be shared on your Facebook, Twitter, Google+, LinkedIn, or Pinterest accounts, and it is there for all your followers to see.

Infographics are an entertaining, educational, and useful tool. They are an integral part of social media marketing and, more importantly, delivers vital information in a fun, engaging, and exciting way.

Infographic Tips for Success

Now that you know a little about infographics and the benefits it provides to businesses, here are few effective tips that can help you to take your visual graphics to the next level.

Tip #1: Foster Creativity and Originality

There are a plethora of visuals and infographics floating on the internet; so, if you want to get yours noticed, make sure to create something original and unique. Invest some time in research and discover what type of topics will most appeal to your target audience. Focus on questions that have been left unanswered and come up with creative ways to answer those questions.

If there is any topic that has already been covered earlier by someone else, but you still want to work on it, make sure you create an infographic with a new and fresh angle.

Tip #2: Know Your Audience

The most essential piece of homework one must do before building an infographic is to find out if it'll actually work with your target audience. Understand the type of topics your audience will prefer and the designs that will appeal to them.

The most suitable tone of the content is also crucial to determine for your audience, as that tone will be used to craft a compelling copy of the infographic. Moreover, also figure out which social media platforms are mostly used by your target audience and create an infographic that performs best on those particular platforms.

Tip #3: Incorporate Attractive Fonts and Colors

Marketers all over the world rely on color psychology and, with its help, produce designs that deliver results. If your infographic does not use fonts and colors to bring your content to life and helps to resonate with the target audience, then it might fail to stand out among other infographics present on the web.

Tip #4: Less Text, More Visual Cues

Using a lot of text can make an infographic seem uninteresting and boring. Therefore, ensure you use a lot of visual cues and a limited amount of text. One way to do this is to supplement or replace labels, subheadings, captions, and other text present in the infographic with images, illustrations, or icons.

Tip #5: Create a Visual Hierarchy

Establishing a visual hierarchy is all about arranging and organizing information on the infographic according to the order or level of importance. That way, viewers can easily scan through from one section to another. Incorporating visual hierarchy can make your infographic look attractive, professional, and cleaner.

Infographics are an excellent way to share complex information in a concise, attractive, and easy to understand way. They are gaining popularity with each passing day, and several businesses have tried to incorporate this tool in their content marketing strategies; some have flourished while others have not. If you want your name to be among the successful, make sure to follow the 'infographic tips for success' shared earlier.

I've included a few infographics throughout this book made both by myself AND I've included a few by SEMrush, with their permission. (Thank you, SEMrush!) Remember your infographics should provide valuable information that your users are in search of.

Side note: Don't forget to download your free resources (which includes some infographics) to further help you with the SEO process at

https://www.beginnersguidetomarketing.com/seo

Part II

Off-Site SEO

Off-Site SEO

A key component to SEO is *off-site SEO*. This is the SEO measures taken *off of your website* to boost your website's SEO. Confusing? I know. That's why we're writing this book to help you understand.

These are some of the items we'll talk about spanning the next couple of chapters:

• Link Building
• Anchor Text
• Negative SEO
• Guest Blogs
• Videos
• Podcasts
• Reviews
• Competitor Analysis
• Local SEO

A large part of your off-site SEO will be building backlinks to your website. SEO is a balancing act. Without hitting all three aspects of SEO (on-site, off-site, technical), your rankings may not do very well, and you'll find that you're simply not very competitive. This section seeks to help you better understand off-site SEO.

Before we get that far however, let's take a closer look at precisely what backlinks are.

Why do I need backlinks?

When your website is new or growing, Google and other search engines may not be sure what your site is about, or even if it can be trusted to have the information in question.

This is where backlinks can help. While there are on-page SEO elements you'll have been working on like creating quality content, using header tags, and other bits and pieces, backlinks are vitally important.

Backlinks are when other websites link to you. They are indicators that you are a trusted source. There are different things to know about backlinks, though. Let's look at how they work and why you need to build the right kind of backlinks to your website.

How do backlinks help you rank?

The more backlinks pointing to your website, the stronger the impact. It says that these other sites find you to be a relevant and helpful site on the given topic.

When they hyperlink to you, if they've chosen "anchor text" or words that your site is about, all the better. It's like a secret handshake with Google, that says, this other site trusts you, and you can trust them too.

Now, it's easy to get caught up in wanting a bunch of backlinks, but not every backlink carries the same weight. It's like when you tell a story, did you get it from the source's mouth? Or was it a story that your grandmother told your brother, and your brother told your mom, now your mom is telling you because your grandmother got the scoop from her neighbor's cousin?

Backlinks that don't come from relevant sources just don't carry the same weight. In fact, if they come from shady places, they can hurt your ranking. You want to make sure that when you're getting backlinks, that they are coming from trusted sources.

There are different ways to get those backlinks, but they aren't always easy. Sometimes it takes solid, link-worthy content like original research or an amazing infographic that people feel compelled to share. Other times, it can be based on an article somebody is writing, and they've linked to your site because it's relevant to their article. Either way, remember, backlinks are good when they come from safe, trustworthy websites that are relevant to your site.

What are citations?

If you're a local site, maybe providing a service, citations are things like your address or phone number that show where you're located. These citations help you show up in local searches. They can be a good strengthener that pulls your site up over another if a person is looking for something near them.

Think about when you do a search for a local restaurant. You'll sometimes see these pop up above regular search listings, because Google is trying to give the user the most helpful answers when they search for "Italian Restaurant in Orlando." If you're an Italian restaurant in Orlando, these citations may even pull up higher than your own webpage listing! Take advantage of these when you can. They're also useful in directories and give you extra backlinks.

Think of national indicators vs. local indicators as an opportunity to be found easier in a specific area.

What is Domain & Page Authority?

Domain authority is a term that was created by MOZ,

a trusted SEO ranking resource. What it means is that the more people that trust your site and link to you, the higher your presence should be when a person searches for a given keyword or phrase. Your domain authority is a number based on a few factors, but generally says how strong your site is based on multiple components.

How this comes into play, is that if you have a couple of websites all vying for first page Google rankings, the domain with the higher authority will most likely rank at the top. It's because with many backlinks pointing to their site, they've proven that they are trustworthy and authoritative in their niche based on outside sources.

Higher page authority simply means that on a trusted website, this particular page is the one that a lot of people point to, because it's got important content. So, while a website might have an overall domain authority score, each page may rank differently. Your About Us page may have a different page authority than the page that goes into the important content that you've highlighted on a quality blog post.

There are a lot of elements that go into website rankings. Each works together with the others to help your website be found. It's important not to neglect them, as they all work as a system. Take out one piece, and you may faulter. SEO is vital if you want to be found in search engines.

Take the Domain Authority as more of a guidelines than a hard truth. It can help you understand areas that you need to improve on, but it is not the end all be all metric of SEO and should **_not_** be taken as such.

Link Building

An essential piece to the <u>SEO</u> puzzle is links. An effective SEO strategy employs link building methods to help drive your company up in search engine rankings. Links are generally divided into three different categories: inbound links, internal links, and outbound links. They can be defined as follows:

Inbound links: Links from another website that points to your site.

Outbound links: Links that direct you to another website.

Internal links: Links used for navigating a website or blog post by linking one page of the website to another page of the same website.

All three types of links are vital to have, but the most coveted are usually inbound links. What exactly are inbound links? And how do they benefit businesses?

What are Inbound Links?

Inlinks, inbound links or backlinks, are all the same thing. It is a simple, essential part of the internet that hyperlinks one webpage to another. Inbound is typically used by the person receiving the link and simply means links that refer back to your blog post or website.

If you've spent even a little time in the SEO industry, you'll know that SEO experts spend their entire careers specializing in gathering links. But why are they so sought-after, and how can you get them?

How Inbound Links Benefit Businesses?

In the SEO industry, usually links equal profits as they drive more traffic to your website and more traffic means more potential users to convert into customers. But why is that? Read on further to learn how inbound links benefit businesses.

Benefit #1: Generate More Traffic

One of the main benefits to inbound links is that it generates more traffic to your website. Of course, more traffic means the more chances you have of converting that traffic into paying customers. Inbound links can help drive traffic to your website through two primary means: By improving SERP ranking and through referral traffic.

Improve SERP Ranking

Inbound links improve the ranking of a business website or blogpost on the search engine result pages (SERP). The higher your website is ranking for certain keywords, the more chances you will have to increase traffic on your web page. The absence of inbound links, in fact, may lower your chances to rank on the search engines (like Google) at all. Therefore, if you want to boost traffic to your website or blog post, make sure you're using inbound links in your SEO strategy.

Referral Traffic

Referral traffic comes from inbound links that direct traffic to your website. When a directory, citation, blog post, etc. links back to your website and users are clicking on that link, they are "referred" to your website by the initial website they found your link on. Hence the term referral traffic.

The volume of traffic received by a referral link depends entirely upon the traffic received by the website or blog post in the first place. If you're looking to work on creating inbound links, you can use tools such as Moz or SEMRush to help you determine how much traffic the website in question is receiving to help determine if the link would be beneficial for you. It is crucial to ensure that you take advantage of inbound links by including information about your website/blog to the linking website. This means that you will generate traffic from your desired target audience, and this the kind of traffic that you can effectively convert into sales.

Side note: When deciding whether a link would be valuable for you, you should also take into account a website's spam score. Google does not place much value in websites that are spammy.

Benefit #2: High-Quality SEO Content

Since the inception of Google's Panda update, the quality of content on a website or blogpost matters considerably more. Those days are bygone when businesses could sprinkle poor quality content on their webpages with phrases and keywords just for the sake of doing it. But now is the era when people want content that has some worth to it. So, what exactly qualifies as high-quality content?

Although there may be several other factors to contend for quality content, it is fair to accept that it embraces the following criteria:

- Creative – content should be interesting, useful and attention grabbing
- Relevant – the material should be relatable to your content

- Unique – it should be unique and not the same tired angle that your competitors are going for

Producing a plethora of content each week is futile until and unless your content is creative, relevant, and unique. To persuade other webpages to backlink to yours, it is vital that you provide *high-quality content* and ultimately escalate the number of quality backlinks to your domain.

Benefit #3: Increase Brand Awareness

Besides boosting your company's SEO strategy, <u>backlinks</u> or inbound links are an excellent way to build and increase brand awareness. Search engines treat quality inbound links as a sign of approval for another source. For example, if The New York Times or other authority website, backlinks to your domain, it indicates to Google that your web page is a source of relevant, legitimate, and credible information. This ensures that you climb the SERP ladder and foster brand awareness among your target audience.

By improving inbound links, businesses can show that they have done the research to find authoritative and credible pages. Moreover, <u>social media</u>, along with other marketing techniques, serve as a way of demonstrating authority within your industry or niche.

Benefit #4: Stay Ahead of Competition

Another key benefit provided by backlinks is to stay ahead of your competitors. Building inbound links improves your standing against other major players present in your niche industry.

For instance, if you are endorsing a service or product

that is very niche, getting another player of the industry to backlink to your webpage can do wonders to put you ahead of your competitors. In a way, those links serve as an endorsement of your website.

Improving inbound strategy can significantly expose your business to a broader target audience.

How to Get Inbound Links?

Now that you know the significance of inbound links, you may be wondering how to get them. So, what is the secret behind receiving a ton of high-quality inbound links?

Although there are several tips and tricks to boost the number of links directed to your website, you cannot escape the hard truth. To generate a successful link-building strategy, a significant amount of time and hard work is required. A couple of common ways to build inbound links include:

1. Develop new high-quality content that is interesting, creative, informative, and link worthy.

2. Try getting backlink references by publications, industry leaders, and other prominent figures.

3. Get the most out of existing links. Make sure the links are operational and not broken.

4. Leverage existing relationships because chances are if any publication uses your backlink, then you both might have familiar audiences.

5. Collaborate with industry thought leaders, organizations, networking groups, peers, etc. to further optimize your link building strategy.

These are only a few of the many ways you can get inbound links. Just ensure that you are producing quality content that aligns with your brand. If readers enjoy the content, chances are they will keep coming back for more.

Inbound links are a valuable component of SEO, therefore, try to build links that entail quality and provide genuine value to your target audience. Adding links just for the sake of it can make matters worse instead of flourishing it.

White Hat versus Black Hat Link Building

Because there is such a thing and it's important to note that those that use black hat link building methods are a ticking time bomb essentially. What I mean by that is this, it's only a matter of time before Google discovers what they're doing and will penalize the poop out of them. Before we get too far in, let's define what white hat link building and black hat link building is.

White Hat Link Building

White hat link building is where you build links back to your site that are considered low risk and that fall within the webmaster's guidelines (Google, Bing, Yahoo, etc.). Through using these methods, you are significantly less likely to be penalized by Google or the other search engines. You don't want any spam penalties!!! The draw to white hat link building, however, is that it is a timely endeavor, one in which some do not have the patience for and turn to black hat link building - or even a gray hat method.

Black Hat Link Building

Black hat link building consists of techniques to gain links for your website that *directly violate webmaster guidelines*. These techniques are often comprised of finding ways to exploit algorithm loopholes in order to rank higher.

While it may be tempting to seek out some black hat link building to give your SEO a quick boost, the long-term effect can be crippling. Instant gratification will not bring about long-term success.

Buying links **goes against Google's webmaster guidelines**. So, don't do it.

Facing Google Penalties

The two main types of penalties Google can slap on your website consists of:

1. Manual penalties
2. Algorithmic penalties

A *manual penalty* means that a member of Google's web spam team (like an *actual* person and not a bot) applied a penalty to your website after determining that your site was in violation of its guidelines. A manual penalty can range in reasons from on-site to off-site, but they do find and penalize those who are using black hat link building techniques.

An *algorithmic penalty* is when a penalty is automatically applied by the bots who are crawling your website which may have discovered a problem with your website. An algorithmic penalty is usually more to do with an on-site issue and not as much to do with shady link building practices.

Removing the Penalty

Yes, it is possible to have Google remove the penalty, but you'll need to fix the issue first before you can file for a reconsideration. Typically, Google wants to see 1) what steps you've taken to correct the issue, 2) how you plan to not engage in this practice again, and 3) provide clear and concise evidence for both #1 and #2.

If you were slapped with an algorithmic penalty, you may need to file a request for reconsideration with Google that we discussed a moment ago, but there's a chance that it may be resolved faster and easier than that. If you've gone in and corrected the issue, the next time the Google bots crawl and index your website, they may remove the penalty. This is not true in all instances of an algorithmic penalty, so be mindful of that moving forward.

Either way, if you've engaged in black hat link building and have been hit with a penalty, you can bet your bottom dollar that your SEO is going to take a HUGE hit. So, when considering taking shortcuts for that instant gratification, you need to ask yourself this: Can you afford a penalty?

Anchor Text and Backlinks

What is it? No, seriously, what is it? All right, you got me. I'm just kidding. Am I allowed to do that in the book?

Anchor text refers to the clickable, hyperlinked words appearing on websites. It can benefit both the search engines in determining what your website is all about as well as users as it provides contextual information about your page/site. Check it out:

Prepare Your Website for the Google Update

There's no denying that the importance of providing your website visitors with an optimal user experience, and the necessity for it is only going to become that much more vital.

If you love a website and everybody else loves that website too, then Google would eventually ensure that the website ranks high on the search result. On the flip side, if everybody feels a site has a terrible user experience, then Google would not rank that site as high on search results in the long run.

Just like any other algorithm update Google does, you should expect to see multiple revisions of Google's new page experience signal over time. Thus, avail the opportunity and fix any usability issues you might have.

Do you see the blue underlined words there "algorithm update"? This excerpt is from a blog on the Pendragon Consulting website and those hyperlinked words are called *anchor text*. When you click on it, it will take you to another article we wrote on our website pertaining to Google algorithm updates. So, you see, the words "algorithm update" fit the content it's hyperlinked to.

What would *not* make sense in this case is if we were to hyperlink to a social media marketing services page or other completely unrelated topic.

Let's walk through a hypothetical situation here. If we were looking to build inbound links to our website, we may seek out opportunities such as guest blogging. Normally, websites that allow you to post a guest blog on their website will allow you one or two links to your website. Those links will not display as your URL (www. pendragonconsultingllc.com) but would rather show as anchor text which would link to your website.

To really get the most benefit from anchor text, you want to try to get the anchor text to match the keywords you'd like your page to rank for. So, if I'm linking back to my homepage (www.pendragonconsultingllc.com) I might want the anchor text to be "Digital Marketing Agency in Maryland", for instance.

Now, you can't always control the anchor text that people are using to link to your website/content. If you're creating valuable content, people will naturally want to link to your content without you prompting them to. Let's look at the different types of anchor text.

Backlinks

These hyperlinks back to your website are also known as *backlinks*. There are two types of backlinks: *no-follow* and *do-follow*. You can probably guess what the difference is here, but we're going to walk through it anyways.

A *no-follow* link tells Google and other search engines NOT to take that particular link into account when determining SEO for either the page the link exists on or the page it's linking to.

A *do-follow* link tells Google and the other search engines to give SEO credit to the page it's linking to. *Do-follow* links are what you want to aim for, though it's not always possible/feasible. If you are keeping track of your Domain Authority (DA), a backlink on a quality website can help you improve your DA score.

Types of Anchor Text

- Exact Match
- Phrase Match
- Partial Match
- Related
- Branded
- Naked URL
- Random/Generic
- Image Links

Exact Match

If you're lucky enough, the anchor text that others use may be an exact match to the keywords you're looking to rank for. (Think back to our Digital Marketing Agency in Maryland example.)

Phrase Match

This is where the anchor text will contain the *phrase* that you're trying to rank for. For example: "Pendragon Consulting a Digital Marketing Agency in Maryland".

Partial Match

This is where the anchor text has all of the words you're trying to rank for, but not the exact phrase, per say. A good example of this is when it's translated into another language.

Related

Related anchor text is when the anchor text is related to the topic in the article and the page the anchor text is linking to but does not necessarily contain the keywords/keyphrases you're trying to rank for. For instance, "SEO is an important part of your marketing strategy." In this example, the SEO would be hyperlinked/our anchor text linking to Pendragon Consulting's website.

Branded

The anchor text is the brand's name. For instance, in our example of "Pendragon Consulting a Digital Marketing Agency in Maryland" only "Pendragon Consulting" would be hyperlinked, making our brand name the anchor text.

Naked URL

Remember how we talked about anchor text isn't typically the URL to your website/webpage? This is the exception. There are times in which your URL will appear on other sites *naked*. That would look something like this: "Pendragon Consulting is a digital marketing agency in Maryland (www.pendragonconsultingllc.com).

Random

This is where the anchor text linking to your website does not contain any branded or relevant keywords but is rather a random hyperlink. You may see it appear like this: "Click here to learn more" with the words "click here" being our hyperlink anchor text.

Image Links

Yup, it is possible for images to have anchor text. The anchor text of an image lives in the alt-text of the image.

Anchor Text and Search Engine Rankings

Just like heading tags, Google and the other search engines use various methods to determine what your page is all about - this includes anchor text. Those external anchor texts help the Google bots determine what your page is all about, leading them to properly classify and index your page and really, your website. If they're confused, it could be cause for your website to be down ranked. Remember, the search engine's goal is to provide an ideal user experience. And that means providing relevant results. If you confuse the search engines, you can bet your bottom dollar that you won't be ranking page one. However, even with some *random* anchor texts here and there that are out of your control, that's not enough for Google's search bots to be confused. With this in mind though, you can see why it's so important to make sure that everything is optimized that you can control (on-site SEO, some of your off-site SEO and your local SEO).

If your anchor text refers to "digital marketing", Google's confidence increases in classifying your page/site as digital marketing and will therefore reward you with a higher rank.

SEO Best Practices for Anchor Text

Now that you know what anchor text is, how can you make sure that you're doing your part to optimize your anchor text?

To ensure that your anchor text is SEO-friendly, you'll want to make sure that keep the following in mind:

1. Length - While there is no defined number of words you can have as anchor text, keeping it to a shorter length (i.e. two to three words or thereabouts) is optimal. However, when determining how many words to use you'll want to keep in mind two things: 1) what is the most accurate way to describe the page you're linking to and 2) what word or phrase would entice users to click on the link?

2. Relevance - We talked about this at the onset of the chapter. Anchor text provides contextual information to both search engines and users. So, if you're linking to a marketing website in an article talking about plumbing, the link is not relevant to the article.

3. Density - It's tempting to go out there and get as many links as you can for the same phrase, linking to the same page to try to get that coveted number one position on Google's Search results. However, thanks to Google's Penguin algorithm update, Google has scrutinized the density of how many times this phrase/link combination appears. If it looks suspiciously like the links did not occur naturally (i.e. you paid someone to place your links there), Google and the powers that be may end up dinging you by marking your website as "spammy".

The exception to this would come under *branded*. If

your brand name, such as Pendragon Consulting, is linked over and over to your website, Google will give the benefit of the doubt and assume that the anchor text is branded (as it is in our example) - though this is not always the case.

Guest Blogging

<u>Blogging</u> is for your own website.

*<u>Guest blogging</u> is when you write an article for **another** website (i.e. third party) and they give you credit for it (and hopefully a dofollow backlink).*

<u>Ghost writing</u> is when you write for someone else's website and don't get credit for it. If you hire a content writer for your website, ensure that your content is all ghost written. To those new to the circle of blogging, MANY businesses turn to content writers to have blogs and the writing on their website professional ghost written and take full credit for it.

Guest blogging is a great way to get your name out there and to build your company's credibility and authority. There's the word authority again. Do you remember we talked briefly about backlinks, inbound links, outbound links and hyperlinks? We talked about it in the chapter on SEO and very briefly in the last chapter if you need a refresher. Guest blogging is an opportunity for gains. These opportunities are not always easy to come by, but if you look hard enough, you'll find them.

So, what is guest blogging? Guest blogging is when you write an article/blog for a third-party website or blog to promote your own company, even if it's just by gaining a backlink. Guest blogging is frequently conducted in content marketing and for SEO purposes.

When should you consider guest blogging? Anytime you're looking for some gains! That's right, I used the word gains. Gains come in the form of quality backlinks to help boost your DA, by helping to establish you as an industry expert and through driving traffic to your website. If the third-party website you're guest blogging on gets a ton of traffic, this *could* greatly improve the traffic to your own website.

If you've decided you want to give guest blogging a go, here are a few things to keep in mind.

- Try to find websites that have at least a Domain Authority (DA) of 30 or higher.
- Every opportunity will present different possibilities.
  - Some will only allow you ONE link back to your website, others may not allow any, but may allow you to mention your company's name in the author bio.
- Guest blogging on another company's website means that you'll likely need to write on a topic that is relevant to their industry, which brings us to the next bullet point.
- Ideal websites for guest blogging should be those within your industry.
- Depending on the website, it can take weeks or even a month or two before you find out if your blog has been accepted for guest blogging and even longer until they post it. Though this is not always the case.
- Some guest blogging opportunities will want your website to have a minimum DA of not less than a certain amount. If your website has a DA of 10 or lower, you may find more no's than yes's.
- It can be frustrating trying to get a guest blog spot, but don't give up. If you wrote a blog for a website that turned down your well-crafted article, repurpose it and post it to your own website. Don't let that content go to waste!!

How to Find Guest Blogging Opportunities

Finding opportunities can prove to be a challenge if you don't know how to find them. Of course, some marketing agencies will offer you a la carte services in which they will write the article for you and get your blog posted. Fiverr also has some who are offering similar. However, why pay boat loads of money when you can do it for free.

Keep in mind that you're looking for *quality* links back to your website and not those riddled with spam and of poor quality. Once you find some opportunities, take a few minutes to check out their Domain Authority on Moz's free tool. It will also tell you their spam score, giving you a clear indication of whether they're worth seeking a backlink from.

Now, to find guest blogging opportunities, go head and open Google (or whatever your preferred search engine is). Now, here's what you want to do. Type in your industry followed by + write for us or + guest blog or + guest post.

So, if I were looking for guest blogging opportunities, I might type in something like this:

Marketing + write for us

Here's what that would look like:

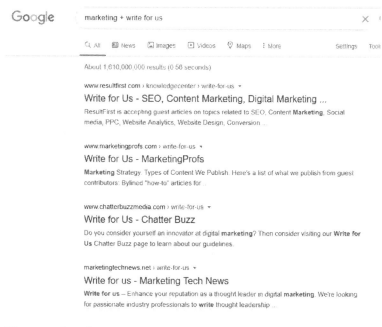

The results that Google returned are all websites that are looking for people to guest post a blog on. Let's say you're a company focused on sales. The same query would apply and look like this:

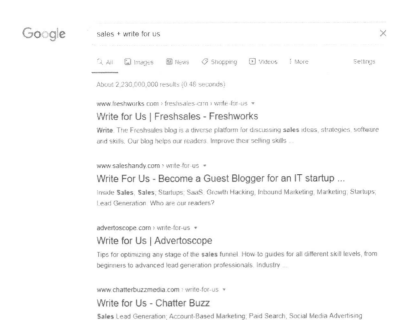

Now that you've found some guest blogging opportunities, check out their DA and Spam score. In this example, we've taken the first result from our marketing + write for us query and plugged it in to see whether they'd be a quality backlink for our site.

Domain Authority	Linking Root Domains	Ranking Keywords	Spam Score
36	2k	1.4k	1%

A DA of 36 certainly isn't considered to be of high authority (we're talking 80's, 90's+), but it can also give you a leg up and a link, so there is nothing to blink at. Their spam score is low and wouldn't *really* be considered a "spammy" website. So, yes, this is a great guest blogging opportunity.

No matter your industry, there's always opportunities out there if you look for them.

Does Social Media Impact SEO?

Not directly, no. However, before you skip this chapter entirely based on my initial answer, there are ways in which social media and SEO can *complement* each other.

Social media signals *do not* have a direct impact on your website's SEO or search engine ranking. However, social platforms are a great way to *amplify* your SEO efforts.

Here are some ways in which you can leverage social media to give your SEO efforts a little boost (not a rankings boost, and not a direct boost):

- Content distribution
- Longer lifespan = more visibility
- Improves visibility & attracts more traffic
- Brand recognition
- Boosts *local* SEO

Content Distribution

If you're here reading this book right now, chances are you're already forming a strategy to implement for your website's SEO success. One of the best things you can do is to create valuable and relevant content for your website. By creating blogs, infographics, videos, etc. you're creating content that others will naturally want to view (driving traffic to your site) and want to link back to (dem backlinks, yo).

Now, without a beautiful page one ranking, traffic to your content may be on the lighter end. One way that you can amplify these efforts is by pushing your content out to social media. By providing the link to your blogs, your infographics, etc., you're giving those following you on social media a heads up that you've just created content that is worth their time to read/view/watch. Through harnessing the power of hashtag research on platforms like Twitter and Instagram, you can take those efforts beyond just your followers to those who may be following those hashtags giving you a much larger audience.

Longer Lifespan

One of the perks of social media is that your content has a longer lifespan. Things get "pinned" over and over and over on Pinterest. Content gets shared for longer periods of time. Of course, the longer the lifespan, the more value you get out of it as well as its continuing to get your name out there, build brand awareness and to drive traffic to your site.

Improves Visibility

Over 70% of adults in the United States are on Facebook - and that's *just* Facebook, not even taking into account any other social platforms. By taking your brand to social media, you can help improve your company's visibility and drive *more* traffic to your website. More traffic means more conversions. (And if it doesn't for you, then maybe you need to make some adjustments to your website to improve the copy, design, UX, etc.)

Brand Recognition

As you work to improve your brand visibility, you'll

also be working to build brand recognition. One of my favorite social channels on LinkedIn is SEMrush. Their content is always on point. I love their infographics. Their infographics, all have a similar color scheme, design and of course, include their logo. If you've been following them on social media, you can easily recognize a SEMrush graphic. They have worked hard to build brand recognition and it shows. This is something we should all be aiming to achieve - brand recognition.

Boost Local SEO

If you have a physical shop location where you can meet your customers, you can add your address to most social platforms. This will help further your *local* SEO. Take a moment to query Google for your company's name (if you've included your address on your social profiles) and look at the results on the first two pages. Normally, you can find at least a listing on page one containing your Facebook profile and in the description under the title tag, you'll find your city, state.

Podcasts

How would you define an audio podcast to someone who has never heard of them before? This question has often surfaced on various social media platforms, including Facebook. Interestingly, but perhaps not surprisingly, the answers varied quite a bit. Although the way people define what an audio podcast differs, the responses generally overlap in the following areas:

- Radio talk
- On-demand
- Free audio shows
- Niche

So, what is a podcast?

For an awesome example, check out my podcast The Beginner's Guide to Marketing (and while you're there, don't forget to subscribe). The podcast is available on most major outlets where you listen to your favorite tunes, podcasts, etc., such as Apple Podcasts, Google Podcasts, Spotify, Anchor.fm, Overcast, etc. Here's the link to Spotify:

https://open.spotify.com/
show/5WTlXgJU6JBqbbIofVWSj2

What are Audio Podcasts?

I'm not sure how many people are aware of this, but the word 'podcast' is actually a portmanteau of iPod and Broadcast.

Audio podcasting came into being as mostly an

independent way for people to get their message out in the world and essentially build a community of individuals with mutual interests. But today podcasts have been adopted by several organizations, big and small, radio networks, comedians, TV networks, churches, storytellers and so much more.

There is not a predetermined or pre-planned length, style, production level, or any particular format of podcasts. They can be split into small episodes or seasons like what we see in a TV show or a serial.

Weekly releases of new episodes are standard, but podcasts can be released be daily, bi-weekly, monthly, or really any cadence the creator desires. In short, podcasts are generally a series of episodes.

These audio files or episodes are stored with a podcast hosting company. One of the best things about podcasts is that listeners can easily subscribe to podcast channels and get notified when the new episode comes out.

Podcasts are not only exciting, but they are also relatively cheap and easy to produce, and anyone can benefit from the growing popularity of podcasts. You can talk about anything, or any topic that interests you and the best thing is you don't have to rely on the radio station for its recording and broadcasting.

4 Benefits of Podcasts for Businesses

Businesses and brands can use podcasts for multiple reasons, such as sharing information about a new service or product, create brand awareness, generate more traffic, or foster relationships with the audience through engaging podcasts. Incorporating podcasts into the marketing strategy can provide several benefits to your business. Read on further to know a few of these benefits:

Fun Way to Drive Traffic

Podcasting can allow businesses to enhance their audience to reach efficiently and quickly. This can help the company to build familiarity with a wide range of listeners. Generally, people subscribe to a podcast channel, and the chances are that as long as the audio episodes keep coming out, the audience will quite likely listen to at least some of it.

In addition to this, podcasts can also help to drive referral traffic towards your business as many listeners recommend and share podcast channels with other people who share similar interests. Thus, this can significantly aid in the company's audience reach.

Foster Connection with The Listeners

Despite being a one-sided medium, podcasts are highly effective in building relationships and connections with the audience. The listeners often feel a close connection to the person speaking on the podcast as they listen to people that share a mutual interest or common notions.

This can allow brands to build valuable relationships and foster trust; thus, listeners can be encouraged to associate themselves with the brand and lead to improved conversion rates as people are more likely to purchase something from a brand that they know something about rather than a complete stranger.

Simple Way to Increase Brand Awareness

The consistency and familiarity of regular audio podcasts can help businesses to make their brand a household name. Businesses can integrate and relate the information about their services and products to the content of the podcast.

For instance, if you're a financial planner, then produce a podcast about stock investing or maybe retirement planning; and incorporate information about the services that you offer in that specific area. This way, podcasts can serve to be a medium of advertisement for your business.

Source of Additional Income

Connecting to the audience can help businesses to open more doors for the target audience to buy their products or services. Additionally, podcasting also proves to be a new source for generating additional income for the company, if the company's podcast channel is successful in acquiring sizable followers. Podcast channels that have significant followers receive sponsorships or payments by other brands for advertisement purposes.

These are just a few of the many benefits of podcasts for businesses. Thus, do not wait any longer and start your podcast channel today!

SEO Benefits of a Podcast

As a form of content, you may be wondering just how podcasts can help you rank in the search engines - because it can. Here's how you can boost your SEO while living that podcast life.

Your podcast will likely focus around one or two topics. Try to select the most *relevant of keywords* pertaining to the topic, just like you would in blog writing. (Do you see where we're going with this?) Once you've identified your keywords, the next step is to write about each episode. Now, there are a few ways in which you can do this.

1. Transcription
2. Blog Writing
3. Hybrid

Transcription

Not quite a hybrid, one of this author's favorite podcast's is by a company called Rank Ranger and is focused on transcription. In addition to writing regular blogs and content, they also have a podcast. In addition to the audio clip, they also provide a "here's what you can expect" overview, followed by a transcription of the entire podcast. This helps them ensure they're content is not only getting out there but is helping their SEO and search engine rankings. Feel free to check out their blog section to get an understanding of what we're talking about:

https://www.rankranger.com/blog

Blog Writing

If you were to go the route of writing a blog on the podcast episode, you'll want to ensure that you're employing SEO formatting with your heading tags, keywords, alt-text and meta descriptions. In addition to proper formatting, you should make sure your blog post has a minimum of 300 words, but preferably no lower than 500 words. This is a short but sweet recap of the podcast episode that can help your rank.

Hybrid

In the hybrid method, you're looking at writing a blog, but using quotes from the transcription to cut down on the amount of writing you'll need to do.

Bonus Tip: Maximize Your SEO Success with YouTube

Second only to Google, YouTube is the second most trafficked site out there with over 1 Billion users. Ensuring that your podcast makes it to your website for SEO and traffic purposes is great, but you can really maximize your success and exposure by also getting your podcast out there on YouTube. It is both free and easy to accomplish.

Effective Podcast Tips for Success

There are a million reasons to get your podcast started today, and not a single reason not to. Having said that, there's a big difference between producing a podcast nobody listens to and producing a successful podcast that can help you with branding, marketing, and maybe even earn some big bucks.

Therefore, here are our top tips to produce and launch a successful podcast.

Tip #1: Get Decent Equipment

The initial investment in equipment is relatively insignificant as compared to the probable gains. But that does not mean you have to spend thousands of dollars on cutting-edge equipment or software. Still, you should at least have a decent microphone, a headset, and some essential editing software to ensure your podcast sounds professional and clear.

Tip #2: Choose the Right Podcast Theme

The theme of a podcast can play a vital role in determining its success. Choose a theme that you not only care about but can also commit to for the long haul. If you're genuinely passionate about what you're speaking, it will resonate with other individuals who share the same thoughts. Being genuinely interested and informed in what you choose to talk about will keep the audience engaged and the listeners will appreciate you for it.

Tip #3: Find Balance

After launching your podcast, you'll probably start receiving suggestions and comments from the listeners. Some might want you to change the format, others might request for special guests; although it is always wise to listen to the needs of the audience, it is equally important to stay true to your identity. Therefore, be in control of the podcast and steer it in the direction that can spark real conversations rather than uninteresting content. Having said that, this does not mean that you completely ignore the wishes of the listeners. Find a balance between your podcast style and the recommendations or suggestions to successfully deliver content that is both loved by you and the audience.

If you are interested in tuning in to our podcast, we've

created a super easy way to get there. Here's the QR code so you don't need to type the entire link in:

Video Marketing

Video marketing has exploded over the past few years, and it is only going to escalate in the future. Several research pieces have shown that people retain 20 percent of what they read, 10 percent of what they hear, and 80 percent of what they see.

Videos, when used in the right way, can be a perfect communication tool for brands. If done correctly, it can lead to increased sales, website traffic, and consumer engagement.

And the best part is that developing an effective video marketing strategy does not have to be complicated. The key to success is to have a concrete plan and content for your video before you start.

But what is video marketing?

Continue reading this complete guide to video marketing and learn why it is crucial for businesses today to incorporate this tool into their marketing strategy.

What is Video Marketing?

If a picture is worth a thousand words, then how much more valued is a video? That is the foundation of video marketing, a straightforward marketing strategy that incorporates engaging videos into the brand's marketing campaign.

Video marketing is used for a plethora of reasons, from building customer relationships to promoting your product, brand, or service. Moreover, video marketing also serves as a medium to promote customer testimonials, present how-to's, deliver viral content, and live-stream events.

In simple terms, when a brand uses a video to market its product, brand, or service, educates current or prospective customers, interacts, and engages with them on social media channels, they are said to be using video marketing.

How Video Marketing Works?

The 'how' of video marketing seems pretty simple on the surface: brands develop a video to promote their company, raise awareness of their products and services, drive sales, and foster customer engagement. But in practice, it is a lot more complicated than this. Like many other marketing efforts, meaningful data is required to drive video marketing. Thus, brands must observe and monitor multiple metrics to track customer engagement.

To build your video marketing strategy, you must:

Allocate Resources:

You will be required to designate some budget for the video – decent equipment, a video marketing team or guru, and good editing software– and the time to create it.

Tell Your Story:

Storytelling might have never been as vital as it is in video marketing, thus starting brainstorming. Figure out what stories you want to tell and how you will share them with the target audience.

Engage Audience:

It is not enough to just share your stories; you must also endeavor to foster customer engagement during the process. What will hook your target audience? How will you make the stories interesting?

Shorter is Better:

There is no fixed length for marketing videos, but the rule of thumb shows that shorter is better. Hence, be ruthless with the editing. Cut out anything that is extraneous as attention spans nowadays are short, thus make the best of what you got.

Publish:

Once the video is ready, make sure you publish it far and wide. Embed them on your website, upload on YouTube, and on all your other social media channels.

Analyze: Focus on stats and track metrics to determine which video performs the best and why.

How Video Marketing Benefit Businesses?

Few of the many benefits provided by video marketing to businesses are:

Improved Conversion Rates

Including meaningful videos on a landing page can boost conversion by 80 percent according to HubSpot. Watching a convincing presenter in a video can influence customers› buying behavior and compel a visitor to turn into a lead or turn a convert into a customer, compared to simply reading the same information alone.

Videos for SEO

Search engines keep looking for content that has viewer engagement capacity. Nothing entices more expansive page views than a video. Moreover, YouTube is the second leading search engine behind Google. If you put a video on your website and YouTube, your opportunity and visibility to show up in search engines is significantly increased.

Foster Credibility and Trust

Videos are a great way to create a distinct personality for your brand or company as it enables you to bond and connect with your audience and earn their trust. The more videos a brand has to help inform and educate customers, the more they'll be able to build on that base of trust. And never forget trust translates into sales.

Encourage Social Shares

This is the age of viral videos, and according to HubSpot, 92 percent of mobile video users share videos with other people. This is an excellent opportunity to have fun and show what your brand is all about. This is your chance to have some fun and really show what your company is all about. Thus, come up with video content that is relevant to your target audience.

Video Marketing Tips for Success

Tip #1: Have a Purpose

Video marketing has become so simple to practice that people often forget about the whole point of creating a video. Thus, make sure that your video has a substantial purpose. It can be anything from increasing brand awareness, encouraging sales, highlighting value propositions to increasing web traffic.

Tip #2: Always Include a CTA

Always try to include some introductory text in your videos that should lead to a call to action. CTA's set up the viewer's expectation for the main content of the video. It is an introduction or a tour of the brand, product, or service.

Tip #3: Set a Video Theme

Video marketing is likely to be more successful when each video is based on a single purpose. If you feel you must include more than one topic in a single video, then try to formulate a common thread between all the different issues. Always remember that the video should serve and fulfill one ultimate purpose.

Tip #4: Don't Pitch for Sales

Generally, videos are not the place or the medium to make a sales pitch. If done the right way, the video itself will help to drive sales. But the main aim should be to offer the target audience with clear information they need to understand the product or service and ultimately lead them further into the sales funnel.

Video marketing is an excellent tool for effective communication in this digital age, especially when the span of attention of people is rapidly decreasing.

There are some really great (and affordable) tools out there to help you create some amazing videos from explainers and promotional to whiteboard and cartoons.

Negative SEO

The peril of negative SEO is far-flung but daunting. How easy is it for a rival to wreck your rankings, and how can you protect your website from it? But before we start, let us ensure that we are clear on what negative SEO is and what it isn't.

In the article, we are going to discuss what negative SEO is, how damaging it can be for your website, and what you can do to detect and tackle a negative SEO attack.

What is Negative SEO?

Negative SEO refers to using any malicious and unethical practice aimed at sabotaging a competitor's ranking in search engines. This is commonly considered 'black hat SEO' and for its vindictive nature.

What it isn't – is a sudden drop in your website ranking.

Kinds of Negative SEO

Negative SEO attacks can take up different forms, such as:

- Hacking your website
- Copying the content from your website and distributing it all over the internet
- Building hundreds or thousands of spammy links to your site
- Creating fake social profiles and tarnishing your reputation online
- Directing links to your site using keywords like poker online, Viagra, poker online, porn, and many others
- Eliminating the best backlinks your site has

Why Negative SEO Attacks Can Be Hard to Detect and Prove?

Detecting and substantiating a negative SEO attack is tricky, particularly if a site's backlink profile already contains a myriad of toxic links or the web site's content is poor or lacks quality.

More than often, webmasters who believe they're a victim of negative SEO, do not consider other conditions that could lead to a drop in their rankings, such as:

- Getting riddled out by Google's algorithmic filtering
- An update in Googles Core Algorithm
- Often, these rank drops are mistakenly taken for negative SEO. So, *what should you do*?

Answer: To avoid any probable adverse impact of updates in algorithms and algorithmic filtering, you must always ensure that the quality of the content you are producing matches <u>Google›s guidelines</u>. Moreover, ensure that you're looking after your backlink profile.

You must understand that auditing your site backlinks is highly critical since you might already have a backlink profile that Google is filtering and perhaps consider it spammy (inclosing unnatural links).

Therefore, numerous webmasters fail to assess these factors and conclude straightaway that their site experienced a negative SEO attack.

Read ahead to learn about some foolproof *'negative SEO protection tips'* for your website.

7 Negative SEO Protection Tips

Tip #1: Set up your Google Webmaster Tools email alerts

This is an excellent way to protect your website from any malicious negative SEO attacks. By setting up your website to Google Webmaster Tools, Google will be able to send you email alerts when:

- Your pages aren't indexed
- Your site is being attacked by malware
- You receive a manual penalty from Google
- You have server connectivity issues

If you have not set up your site already, connect your site to Google Webmaster Tools now!

Tip #2: Regularly monitor your link profile growth

Preventing a negative SEO attack is not something that is in your power but detecting the attempt early enough to rear the damage is very much possible. For this purpose, you should regularly monitor your link profile growth.

For instance, platforms like SEO SpyGlass provide you progress comprehensive graphs for both the number of referring domains and the number of links in your profile. An unusual surge in either of these graphs is a good enough reason to look into the links you precipitously acquired.

Tip #3: Always keep track of your backlinks profile

Apart from keeping an eye on the increase in your profile links, it is equally important to keep track of your backlinks all the time, whether there's an increase or decrease. It can be one of the most critical actions to prevent spammers from succeeding.

Mostly, they perform negative SEO against your site by building redirects or low-quality links. It's enormously crucial to know when someone is producing links or redirects to your site. You can use tools like Open Site Explorer or Ahrefs, from time to time, to check if somebody is building links to your site.

Tip #4: Regularly screen your social media mentions

Sometimes, spammers would create fake profiles on social media platforms by using your website or company name. Therefore, regularly screen your social media mentions and try to remove these accounts by reporting them as 'spam' before they get any followers.

To figure out who's exploiting your brand name, you can use platforms like Mention. Whenever somebody mentions your brand name on any social media platform, you will be notified, and then you can decide if you want to take any action or not.

Tip #5: Avoid making enemies online

You must understand that there's no reason to form enemies online. Do not ever argue with customers or clients because you never know who you're dealing with. There are three reasons why they would spam your website:

- To outrank the competition in search engines
- For revenge
- For fun

Tip #6: Keep an eye on duplicate content

One of the most common methods a spammer uses is content duplication. They duplicate your site's content and post it wherever they can. If most of your website content is replicated, there is a massive probability that your site will be penalized and eventually lose rankings.

You can see if your site has duplicate pages on the web with the help of Copyscape.com. Simply add your site URL or the body of the content you want to verify, and it'll show you if it has been published somewhere else on the internet without your permission.

Tip #7: Do not be prey to your own search engine optimization strategies

Ensure you're not hurting your website rankings by using tactics that aren't acceptable to Google. Here are a few of the things you shouldn't do:

- Do not purchase links at all for SEO
- Do not purchase links from blog networks,
- Do not link to penalized sites.
- Do not publish a myriad of low-quality guest posts.
- Do not create too many backlinks to your site using 'money keywords.' Remember, at least 60 percent of your anchor texts must involve your site name.

Detecting and undoing negative SEO is daunting, but it is not impossible. Therefore, keep these negative SEO protection tips in mind if you ever notice your search engine website ranking deteriorating.

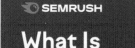 

What Is Negative SEO?

Negative SEO—a "black hat" tactic aimed at sabotaging a competitor's website search rankings.

Negative SEO types

⚡ Hacking a website

⚡ Creating toxic backlinks with spammy anchor texts pointing to the website

⚡ Scraping a website's content and creating duplicates of the website

⚡ Posting fake negative reviews

⚡ Creating toxic backlinks with spammy anchor texts pointing to the website

⚡ Removing the website's backlinks by sending out fake removal requests to webmasters

How to prevent a Negative SEO attack

☑ Set up alerts in Google Search Console

☑ Perform regular site audits for technical issues

☑ Perform regular backlink audits

☑ Perform regular duplicate content audits

☑ Use the Disavow tool for spammy looking backlinks

☑ Monitor online reviews for legitimacy

☑ Avoid thin content by creating unique, engaging & helpful content

Spotting and proving a Negative SEO attack is tricky

Here's how you can differentiate.

What is NOT Negative SEO

🔍 An existing backlink profile containing many toxic backlinks

🔍 Organic ranking drops due to algorithm changes or filters

🔍 An increase in negative reviews from legitimate customers

Possible signs of a Negative SEO attack

🔍 Hijacked website

🔍 Changes to robot.txt or sitemap

🔍 An significant increase in spammy backlinks & lost or removed quality backlinks

🔍 Cloned website or content

🔍 Spotting mass fake negative reviews

SEO Competitor Research

You may not be a competitive person (or maybe you are), but when it comes to SEO, you either compete or forfeit. There is no in between here. Ranking for keywords is super competitive. And in order to be truly effective at ranking for those keywords that can make or break you, you need to know who the competition is.

Here's what we're looking for:

- Who are your *actual* SEO competitors?
- What keywords are they ranking for? And how much traffic are those keywords bringing in?
- What topics are they covering and how much traffic do those topics bring in?
- Who is linking to my competitors? And can you get a link from those sites as well?
- Let's take that one step further…
- What social channels are my competitors marketing on?
- What is their social following size?
- How much engagement do they have?

Using that information, you can create a plan to help you rank higher, faster. Sounds like spying, right? Your ethics will not be called into question by "spying" on your competitors because we're all out there spying on each other in terms of SEO. And you better believe that your competitors are 100% spying on you.

Tools for SEO Competitor Research

There are some really GREAT tools out there, many of

which offer free trials. When I start out with new projects, I love taking new tools for a test drive. You may be happy with the tools that you're familiar with, but there could also be something even better out there that you're missing out on. Here are some of the tools I'd recommend checking out to help you "spy" on the competition:

- SEMrush
- Ahrefs
- Spyfu
- Moz

Channel Your Inner Yogi Bear

Because we're about to go steal some picnic baskets :D

If you don't know who Yogi Bear is, I'm not sure we can be friends haha.

All right, armed with your tool of choice, here's what you want to scope out. *I'll be using Moz's _free_ link explorer tool as we walk through this next part.*

Who is Your Competitor?

No, it's not that big brand with a big budget. It's going to be a company who has similar offerings to yours and is similar in budget. As a small to mid-sized business, saying that large brands are your competitors is like a drop in a bucket, and you my friend, are the drop. In the bucket. Unless you are also a large brand with deep pockets.

Now, let's take another look at who your competitor is. I sat down a client who owns a process serving company here in Maryland. We did a little bit of competitor research and he wanted to go broad, looking at 1) nationally and

2) chains. He is a small business owner with a single location. Neither of those would necessarily fit the role of "competitor". So, what we did was because he has a physical location and a well-defined service area (i.e. not selling products or services nationally or globally, but rather within a specific geographic area) is that we looked at Google Maps.

From Google Maps we were able to take a look at 5 - 10 websites and narrow down his competition to the top 3. We then took those top 3 results and plugged the URL (one by one) into Moz's Link Explorer tool. In here, we were able to see the top keywords they were ranking for, their Domain Authority (DA), their recent links (including *who* is linking to them) and a few other bits.

The How

We were able to compile that list of keywords into one document and then, I like to use SEMrush for my keyword research, we plugged them in there to identify the monthly search volume for the keywords they were ranking for as well as the competition score. Remember, we're looking for those *long-tail keywords* and not broad keywords that are difficult to rank for.

Once we identified some keywords that were valuable, we then formed a strategy. In addition to writing some new content for his site, we were also going to go back through and spruce up some of his current content to include those keywords.

Now, who is linking to them? Moz will give you the last 90 days of gained and lost links in their free Link Explorer tool. If you want more than that, you'll have to pay to upgrade on their site or use another tool to check out their links. Any of the tools mentioned above can get the job done.

There are good links and bad links. Good links are those directory listings that can help improve your *local SEO* and they are links related to your industry, niche, profession, etc. If you push a press release, you'll notice a number of backlinks (if you've included a backlink in the article provided for the press release). Those are great as well.

However, there will be some links that you'll come across at some point that are less than savory and downright spammy. Avoid them. Seriously, it's not worth the penalty that Google could slap on your site.

If you run the links you're looking at potentially getting listed on through Moz's Link Explorer tool, it will show you the spam score. Be mindful of that number as you move forward with getting listed on their website.

By this stage, you should have identified 1) who your *SEO* competitors are, 2) what keywords they're ranking for, 3) which keywords would be beneficial for your site, 4) built a list of their links and 5) identified from that list, which links would be worth reaching out to in order to get your own site listed, the next step is to dig into their content.

What type of content is your competitor building on? Are their blogs crushing it? Are they focused on 2-3 particular focal areas instead of everything? How can you shape your content around what they're doing?

And it's not about copying what they're doing. In fact, it is heavily frowned upon to plagiarize. Just going to throw that out there to get that out of anyone's mind before it even takes a trip down that alley. Google will penalize duplicate content. And it's just plain dirty. Don't do it.

However, you can take a look at several items to help you shape your content around what they're doing. Here's what we're looking for:

- What is the topic about?
- What keywords are important (multiple iterations of the keyphrases)?
- How many words does the article have?
- Have they broken their article down using lower-level subheadings with the appropriate heading tags?
- How much traffic is the article getting?
- Who is linking to this article?
- Where does the article rank on the search engines?

One tool that I absolutely LOVE is Surfer SEO. I talked about it in my book on Content Marketing, and I'll talk about it again because I love it that much.

If you sign up for an account with them, you're able to create your content directly in their "Content Editor". You choose the topic and prime keywords you're focused on and it will literally do all of the hard work for you. It tells you everything from who the top 10 sites are that are ranking on page for your specified topic/keywords, what keywords your blog should include and how many times they should be in your article, what the minimum recommended word count is based on those top 10 rankings, and so much more. You also have the ability to look at who is linking to those top 10 websites so that you can reach out to them for a backlink as well.

SurferSEO also has a free Chrome extension you can download called Keyword Surfer. This plugin will show you an *approximate* monthly search volume for the keyword(s) you type into Google. One of the things I really love about this plugin is that you can also see (just from this plugin) related searches AND a chart showing the word count and number of links each of the top results have. This gives you an idea of whether you'll be able to compete for it and if so, how many words you'd need to write to be competitive.

Yet another way of conducting competitive research.... Kind of in reverse.

Let's say that you've conducted some keyword research and you want to rank for a specific phrase. What you could do is type it into Google using your Keyword Surfer extension to analyze the top competition for that keyword/phrase. I wouldn't use this in place of competitor research that we talked about above, but rather for keyword ranking and a quick peek into things.

Are you ready to break out your handy dandy notebooks and spy goggles yet?

Integrating Local SEO

Local SEO is another area you should be particularly mindful of if you have a physical shop/office that your customers can visit. What local SEO can do is help improve your search visibility in your *local area*.

Before we dive too deep into the nitty gritty, I'd like to pause and ask you to head over to Google and query your company's name. The Search results should return a bunch of different websites (including your own). How many of those websites, have you claimed your profile on? There will be some unrelated results that return but go through let's say the first five pages on Google. This will end up being your starting point.

There are probably a bunch of websites in those results that you didn't even know your company was listed on. What you can do is then go in and "claim" those listings, providing them with your correct contact information and address. These will all play a role in your *local SEO*.

What is Local SEO?

Local SEO is just that - optimizing your website for *local* traffic. If you're a financial advisor, you're likely looking for clients in a specific location. You wouldn't be looking for clients in another state necessarily. Local SEO would be getting your company listed in local directories to prove that you're legitimate as well as improve your local ranking. Just like regular search results, places like Google Maps also has a ranking algorithm for local searches and of course, you want to be one of the top results to drive more traffic to your business.

If we were to query the search engines (Google in this example) for "financial advisor in Annapolis, MD" this is what might show:

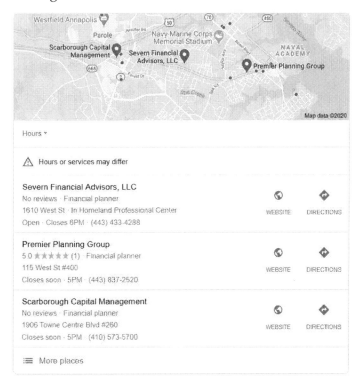

Those three results are in the coveted top three positions and are likely to receive the bulk of traffic from that query. How did they get there? SEO, my friend.

NAPs and Local SEO

No, it's not a nap as much as we all probably wish it was. (Maybe it's just me wishing for a nap) There are a lot of marketing acronyms out there and if you're not in the marketing industry, they may not make a whole lot of sense. Let's dig a bit deeper here.

What is NAP?

When discussing marketing, the term NAP stands for Name, Address and Phone Number. NAPs are one of the fundamental components to high visibility in local search results (i.e. ranking higher on Google or other search engines for local goods or services). A good example of a NAP citation would be <u>social media</u>. On Facebook, the About section normally has the business' contact information:

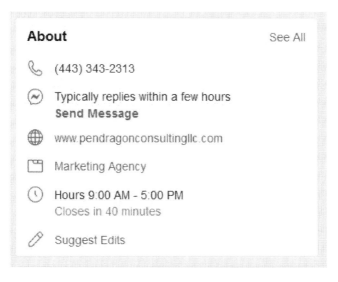

A citation is a listing on a website or directory that contains the NAP of a business. There are times which the citation may also contain more information, such as a website. This is the case in our Facebook example above.

There are some websites that scrape your information

from other sources such as your website or other listings to create an entry on their own website with your information. If your business has been around for a while, I guarantee you have listings you didn't even know existed. Try to carve out about 30 minutes (or less) to go through the first 5 - 10 pages of Google (or other search engine) after you've queried your company's name. Look at each listing to see if there are issues with any of your NAPs, if there are, you'll want to get them fixed.

Benefits of Having Accurate NAPs

You may be wondering if it's really *all that* important if one or two results have inaccurate information. Outside of potentially losing business because of incorrect information, it can also harm your legitimacy and cause the search engines to <u>downrank</u> your website.

The first impression a potential client gets from your business shouldn't be inaccurate contact information. Unless there's a very specific reason for choosing your company, many aren't going to chase up the *correct* contact information but will rather choose your competitor instead. And let's face it, bad information can leave a bad impression.

The search engines have a complex algorithm. It the search bots come across multiple addresses, names or phone numbers it will be confused by which information is accurate and therefore, downrank your website. Your on-site and off-site SEO game might be strong, but without accurate NAPs, you're not doing yourself any favors.

Cleaning up and building those local citations can be both time consuming and rewarding. If you're willing to put in the work, the reward can be exponential.

Here are a few tips out of many that can help you get started on the right foot with local SEO.

Optimizing for Local SEO

Google My Business

If you consult any digital marketing professional, this will be the first advice they'll give you. Google My Business is a way small businesses can verify their business's presence on Google as authentic.

You can optimize your Google My Business page with the correct address, website link, phone numbers, hours of operation, the exact location you serve (multiple locations if you are based in different areas) etc. You can even post to Google My Business, just as you would on social media. If you don't have a Google My Business set up yet, this should be your first stop.

Optimizing Meta Details and Content

The URL of your website, the content you post on it and each web page's title, headers, meta descriptions, alt-text etc. are all opportunities for optimizing your content for local search engine results pages (SERPs).

The process of optimization is similar to traditional SEO with the addition of geo-targeted keywords.

Another way to use content for local SEO is by adding **location pages** if you have multiple physical stores and/ or an online business that serves particular localities. Not only will you have more pages for Google to index and rank but the addition of location-based keywords and content with details regarding your store, parking situation, nearby location, address and phone number etc. will drive more localized traffic.

Online Directories

Yes, virtual Yellow Pages do exist. You can list your business on these directories based on your location, gaining an additional source of traffic diversion. Additionally, map aggregating platforms such as My Business Listing Manager are also effective options. I personally like to use a platform called BrightLocal to help build and maintain listings.

One thing to make sure when listing your business is to ensure all information is correct across all citations. There should be no discrepancies – even in spellings – or Google might not rank your page properly.

Getting Inbound Links

The last in this article but certainly not the least, getting inbound links for your website is a great way to build credibility. Google assesses any high-authority inbound links you have on your website, which increase your business's domain authority.

For local SEO, these links can come from licensure bureaus such as the Better Business Bureau, local industry-relevant associations, local government of official agencies, manufacturers, affiliates and more.

Rebranding and Local SEO

If you decide to change the name of your company,

acquire a new URL/domain, change your phone number, your address, etc. those are all things that you will **_need_** to make sure are updated ASAP in your citations.

As you go through and create your citations and local listings, I'd encourage you to keep an excel spreadsheet with the URL, username and password for each of the citations that you've created so that if you ever do update/change any of those important elements, you can easily identify which ones will need to be updated. This is when building and managing your listings through a service such as BrightLocal makes it easier as well as you have every bit of information centrally located and can easily apply any updates to your account to make sure your local SEO doesn't suffer as a result of any inaccurate NAPs.

The practice of local SEO doesn't end here. Considering the vastness of the digital landscape, there are various other ways small businesses can use geo-targeting to gain an increased number of local customers that lead to more sales.

Reviews & SEO

Reviews and SEO have been closely tied for a while now. Though the impact is actually greater to local SEO in this instance.

A question I always ask my clients is this: If you're looking for an Italian restaurant within a 10-mile radius of your location, what do you do? The answers rarely differ. They go to their preferred search engine and query for results. Most search engines will show results in two formats, a list next to a map or links to the business' website *(*cough, cough* local SEO*). Many choose to use the results next to the map to see where specifically the Italian restaurant is located. Scrolling through the results shows you a few things: name, cuisine, location and reviews (if they have any). Let's say there are three Italian restaurants near you. How would you choose which restaurant to eat at? You'd probably turn to the reviews.

Here's what Google has to say on how they determine *local SEO* ranking.

How Google determines local ranking

Local results are based primarily on relevance, distance, and prominence. A combination of these factors helps us find the best match for your search. For example, our algorithms might decide that a business that's farther away from your location is more likely to have what you're looking for than a business that's closer, and therefore rank it higher in local results.

Relevance

Relevance refers to how well a local Business Profile matches what someone is searching for. Add complete and detailed business information to help Google better understand your business and match your profile to relevant searches.

Distance

Distance considers how far each potential search result is from the location term used in a search. If a user doesn't specify a location in their search, we'll calculate distance based on what we do know about their location.

Prominence

Prominence refers to how well known a business is. Some places are more prominent in the offline world, and search results try to reflect this in local ranking. For example, famous museums, landmark hotels, or well-known store brands are also likely to be prominent in local search results.

Prominence is also based on information that Google has about a business, from across the web, like links, articles, and directories. Google review count and review score factor into local search ranking. More reviews and positive ratings can improve your business' local ranking. Your position in web results is also a factor, so search engine optimization (SEO) best practices apply.

Tip: There's no way to request or pay for a better local ranking on Google. We do our best to keep the search algorithm details confidential, to make the ranking system as fair as possible for everyone.

There you have it… straight from the horse's mouth (Google being the horse). Here's the link to view this particular bit of information on their website:

https://support.google.com/business/answer/7091?hl=en

While we all look for those willing to leave a good review, there will at some point, be someone who will leave you a less than stellar review. And that's okay. How you respond will determine how customers will choose to interpret the review and help determine whether they plan to frequent your business.

Bad Reviews

Okay, let's just jump right into the mix here. As I mentioned above, you can't please everyone. We also need to take into account who is most likely to leave a review -- is it someone who received standard service? Or will it be the person who received above or below standard service? That's right. An individual is more likely to leave a review if they've had a phenomenal experience or what they believe was a terrible experience.

Bad reviews can break a business, especially a small business. However, just because someone left you a bad review doesn't mean you just let them have open season bashing your business. You have a powerful weapon in your arsenal… a response. When potential customers are perusing your reviews, they want to see that you're responsive and that you're taking action. Responding to negative reviews can be crucial, especially the right response.

Here are some tips to help you respond appropriately to those negative reviews:

- Address them by name
- Thank them for taking the time to leave a review
- Apologize and empathize
- Personalize your message without being *too* personal
- Take the conversation offline.
- Offer a solution - when you're able to
- Once the situation is resolved, if it gets resolved, ask the customer if they'd be willing to change their review

Lack of Reviews

Chances are, if you're just starting out you may not have many reviews, if at all. It's not the end of the world, but it could definitely mean the difference between a client choosing your competitor's business over yours. There is no harm in asking your clients to leave you a review. Any why not make it convenient for them? Provide links that take them directly to your company's page on Google My Business, Yelp or any other relevant review-based platform. There's even software out there, such as Birdeye, that makes asking for reviews an automated process. It can send your clients an email or text message assisting in the review process and even send reminders and surveys if they weren't very happy. The point is, don't be scared to ask for reviews.

Be a go getter and go get those reviews!

Part III

Technical SEO

Diving into Technical SEO

This is an ultimate, all-encompassing guide to technical SEO for beginners. In this guide, you will learn about:

- HTTPS
- XML sitemap
- Hreflang
- Canonicalization
- Structured data
- Site Speed
- Duplicate versions
- Lots more

If you want to ensure that your technical SEO is up to date, you ought to receive great value from this technical SEO guide.

But first, let's answer the question "what is technical" and why it is still extremely important in 2020.

So, let's dive in!

What Is Technical SEO?

The process of making sure that a site fulfills the technical requirements of modern search engines with the aim to improve organic rankings is known as 'Technical SEO.' Essential elements of Technical SEO include indexing, crawling, rendering, and site architecture.

Why is Technical SEO Important?

You must understand that just having the best content or the best website is not enough to rank on search engines.

It is as simple as this:

If your technical SEO is not up to speed or messed up, you are not going to rank.

At the most rudimentary level, Google and other modern search engines need to be able to discover, crawl, render and index the webpages on your site.

But that is honestly just scratching the tip of the iceberg. Even if a search engine does index all of your website's content, that does not, in any way, mean that your job is done.

Why?

Because, for your website to be fully optimized for technical SEO, your website pages must be secure, fast loading, free of duplicate content, mobile-optimized, and a myriad of other factors that go into technical optimization.

Now, this does not mean that technical SEO has to be flawless to rank – because it does not.

Just remember, the easier you make it for search engines to access your site content, the higher chances you will have to rank.

How to Improve Your Technical SEO?

Like we explained earlier, technical SEO is not just about crawling or indexing. To expand and enrich your website's technical optimization, you should take into account the following elements of technical SEO:

- - HTTPS
- - XML sitemap
- - Hreflang

- - Canonicalization
- - Structured data
- - Site Speed
- - Duplicate versions
- - Lots more

If you do not know what these are, don't fret.

Fortunately, we are going to cover all of these elements in the rest of this guide.

#1: HTTPS

HTTPS or Hypertext transfer protocol secure is the protected or secured version of HTTP, which is the prime protocol used to direct data between a website and a web browser. HTTPS is encrypted to enhance the security of data transfer. This is crucial, particularly when users convey sensitive data, such as by signing into a bank account, health insurance provider or email service.

Any site, particularly those that necessitate login credentials, must use HTTPS. In some browsers such as Chrome, sites that don't utilize HTTPS are marked differently than the ones that are. You should always look for a green padlock in the URL bar to ensure the page is secure.

HTTPS is a critical element of technical SEO because web browsers like Safari, Chrome etc., take HTTPS very seriously; they flag all non-HTTPS sites as not secure because HTTPS prevents sites from having their data broadcast in a way that is easily viewed by anybody snooping on the network.

#2: XML Sitemap

In a nutshell, an XML sitemap is a list of your site's URLs, which acts as a roadmap and tells Google what content is available on your site and how to reach it.

Now, you want search engines to crawl every essential page of your site. But usually, they end up without any internal links directing to them, making it hard for Google to find them.

This is where the role of an XML sitemap comes into play. It lists your site's important pages and ensures that search engines can easily find and crawl them all. Moreover, it also helps Google to understand your site structure.

XML sitemaps can be excellent for Technical SEO, as they allow search engines to rapidly find your important site pages, even if your internal linking is not perfect.

#3: Hreflang

Hreflang is essentially an HTML attribute used to specify the geographical targeting and language of a webpage. If you have numerous versions of the same page in diverse languages, you can utilize the hreflang tag to communicate to Google and other search engines about these variations. This allows them to serve the appropriate version to their users.

Now, hreflang might seem like a simple HTML attribute, but it is one of the most complicated aspects of technical SEO and can be quite tough to get to grips with. Therefore, make sure you are making all the right moves.

Remember, catering to the native language of search engine users improves their experience. This usually results in lesser people clicking away from your page and back to the search results - i.e., higher dwell time - a higher time on page, a lower bounce rate, etc. - all the good things that we believe have a progressive impact on SEO and rankings.

#4: Canonicalization

When search engines crawl the same content on different pages, it sometimes does not know which web page to index in search results. This is why the canonical tag was introduced. It assists search engines in better indexing the favored content versions instead of their duplicates.

The rel= "canonical" tag helps you to tell Google where the master or original version of content is located. You are basically saying, "Hey Google! Do not index this page; instead, index this source page."

So, if you wish to republish a chunk of content, whether slightly modified or exactly the same, but do not wish to risk producing duplicate content, the canonical tag is there to save you.

Correct canonicalization makes sure that each unique piece of content on your site has only a single URL. To prevent Google from indexing various versions of a single page, we recommend you have a self-referencing canonical tag on each page of your website.

#5: Structured Data

Structured data is a standard format to markup web page information and data. It assists search engines like Google, Yahoo, Bing and others to understand better what a web page is about.

When search engines correctly understand the content of a web page, then it can better serve it for fitting search queries. It is also used by search engines in the so-called "rich snippets" to improve the user experience visually.

#6: Site Speed

Site Speed is simply the amount of time a website takes to load. A website's loading speed is determined by many different factors, such as a website's server, image compression and page file size.

That said, site speed is not as simple as it sounds.

Because there are several ways of measuring site speed, here are the three most common:

- **Time to First Byte:** This assesses the amount of time it takes for a webpage to begin the loading process.
- **Fully Loaded Page:** This measures the amount of time it takes for the resources on a webpage to load 100 percent.
- **First Contextual Paint/ First Meaningful Paint:** This measures the amount of time it takes for the load to load enough resources to really view and read the content on your webpage.

You must understand that site speed is a critical element of technical SEO. It is so crucial that Google has made it an actual SEO ranking factor.

#7: Duplicate Content

Duplicate content is simply the content that is an exact copy or similar to the content on other sites or different pages of a single site. You must keep in mind that having huge amounts of duplicate versions of content on your site can adversely affect your Google rankings.

Generally, search engines do not want to rank websites or pages with duplicate content. Instead, they try hard to index and provide a web page with unique or distinct information to users.

Thus, if you have pages on your website that lack distinct information, know that it can significantly hurt your search engine rankings. Moreover, there are few other problems a website with duplicate content often faces:

- - Less organic traffic
- - Fewer indexed pages
- - Penalties (rarely)

It doesn't end there, so go grab a smoke, a drink, some fresh air, whatever you need to do before we continue on with technical SEO.

Improving Website & Page Speed

In the introduction to technical SEO, we talked briefly about the SEO value a speedy website has. As we get closer to the Page Experience update Google is rolling out in 2021, the speed of your website becomes *even more* important. The longer it takes for your site or page to load, the higher your bounce rate will end up as people simply don't want to wait. What this ultimately means is that a lengthy load time could be costing you business.

Let's first clarify something here… Site speed and page speed are two different things. Your site speed is the speed of a sample of page views on your website. Page speed is the "page load time" or "time to first byte" and it's ultimately the amount of time it takes for the *page* to load.

To check out your page speed, you can use the Google PageSpeed Insights tool: https://developers.google.com/speed/pagespeed/insights/

Page load time not only plays an important SEO role - especially in providing an optimal User Experience (UX) - it also can have a significant impact on conversions. Check out these stats by The Daily Egg:

"A one-second delay in page load time yields:

- *11% fewer page views*
- *16% decrease in customer satisfaction*
- *7% loss in conversions*

*A few extra seconds could have a **huge** impact on your ability to engage visitors and make sales." (source: The Crazy Egg)*

Google's Take on Site (and Page) Speed

There are over 200 factors that Google's algorithm uses to determine where your site should rank in its Search Results. Google has actually gone on record to say that site speed *is* actually a ranking factor and they place special importance on it. Once the Page Experience update is rolled out, this will be doubly true. Again, they care about the User Experience (UX) and want to provide the most relevant content providing the most optimal experience for their users. Your website could have great information on it, but if it takes a while to load, you can expect to not rank as well as you could.

Check out Google's claim that this *is* in fact a ranking factor here:

https://developers.google.com/search/blog/2010/04/using-site-speed-in-web-search-ranking

So, what is a good page load time? Google has indicated that three seconds is optimal. However, according to Think with Google, "the average mobile page takes more than 15.3 seconds to fully load". Hopefully when you see that red bit of doom in analyzing your page speed, it spurs you to action, but doesn't give you heart palpitations as many sites are not able to reach that three second objective very easily, if at all.

Tips for Improving Site Speed

While I strive to provide a fair bit of information in my

book, I'm going to also place a link here to an article on CrazyEgg (founded by Neil Patel) as it provides some great information on how to accomplish these tasks and it's another valuable resource that I believe can help you on your SEO journey:

https://www.crazyegg.com/blog/speed-up-your-website/

1. Minify CSS, JavaScript & HTML

2. Reduce Redirects

3. Defer JavaScript Loading

4. Remove Render-Blocking JavaScript

5. Minimize First Time to Byte

6. Harness the Power of Browser Caching

7. Improve Server Response Time

8. Optimize & Compress Images

9. Use a Content Distribution Network (CDN)

#1 Minify CSS, JavaScript & HTML

This is code ladies and gentlemen and for this section, if you don't write code, you may want to consider hiring a developer to assist with this part. Through optimizing your code, you can dramatically reduce lag time and increase your page speed.

If you've run your website through Google PageSpeed Insights, chances are that you will have also seen the "remove unused JavaScript" message in there as well. This is part of this step… you'll want to ensure that you go in and remove code comments, formatting as well as that unused code.

To really understand this one, we need to look at what an **HTTP Request** is. HTTP stands for Hypertext Transfer Protocol. HTTP is the command language that devices follow in order to communicate with one another. Before we continue with this bit of nerdiness, let's take a quick look at how a URL breaks down.

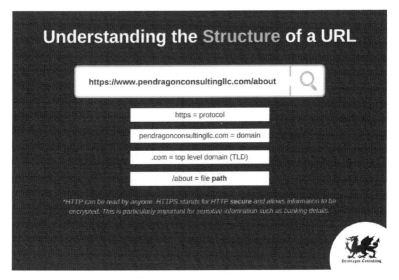

Your URL is similar to your home address or phone number. It is a personal identifier which describes how to reach your business. When people use your identifier to find you by typing in your URL into their browser, let's say on their mobile device, they are making a request. That request can be things such as retrieval or to modify something. In this instance, it is retrieval. The mobile device that the individual is using to find you is the *client* making a GET (retrieval) request.

You'll want to identify which clients (various devices and applications) are making HTTP requests of your website and then, minify/minimize them. You can do this by using your Google Chrome browser's Developer Tools to identify who is making HTTP requests and how often. The link on CrazyEgg we mentioned earlier provides guidance on how to accomplish this.

https://www.crazyegg.com/blog/speed-up-your-website/

Once you've identified who is making the requests and how often, you can begin to minify and combine files. The process of minifying involves removing whitespace, unnecessary formatting and unused code. If you're using WordPress for your website, you can use the WP Rocket plugin to help simplify this process.

#2 Reduce Redirects

Your site load time is vital to conversions. No one wants to wait. Which is why a shorter page loading time is so beneficial to your website. Again, this also goes into Google's Page Experience update rolling out soon…

A redirect is when you visit one page that perhaps no longer exists and you are then *redirected* to another page.

SEMRush has a Site Audit tool that can dig up tons of information on your temporary redirects, redirect chains & loops. You can sign up for their free 7-day trial to give this bad boy a spin. However, if you are going to do their 7-day free trial, I'd encourage you to wait until the end of this book and use it when you're ready to run your SEO audit, which I get into at the end.

#3 Defer JavaScript Loading

For this section, you can also use the WP Rocket plugin

if you have a WordPress website. If you are using this plugin, you'd simply need to check the box "load JS files deferred".

If you have an HTML website, this Varvy link is your friend with some great instructions for placing an external JavaScript file, providing clear, step by step instructions.

https://varvy.com/pagespeed/defer-loading-javascript.html

#4 Remove Render Blocking JavaScript

Before we get too nerdy here, let's talk about DOM, which stands for Document Object Model. The DOM is a cross-platform and language-neutral interface which essentially treats both XML and HTML documents as a tree. This tree structure contains nodes, and those nodes are objects representing pieces of the document.

Before a browser can render a page, they must have built a DOM tree by parsing HTML. Should that document contain any script, the browser will need to stop and execute the script before it can continue rendering the page. This script is also known as *render blocking JavaScript*. Ultimately, Google suggests that you try to avoid, or at least minimize your use of blocking JavaScript. What's important to note here is that "JavaScript resources are parser blocking by default unless marked as "async" or added via a special JavaScript snippet". (Source: Developers.Google.com)

#5 Minimize Time to First Byte

So, the two metrics that we're really looking at when we try to improve our site and page speed is:

1. How long does it take for your page to *fully* load?

2. What amount of time does it take to *start* loading the page? (i.e. time to first byte)

The Time to First Byte (TTFB) is the amount of time it takes to *start* loading your page. How long will the browser need to wait until it receives the first byte of data from the server? This is a metric that you can again, check out in a Google Chrome browser and the Developer Tools. *(See the CrazyEgg link for a quick how-to.)*

Instead of Google Chrome, you can also use this site as well to check your TTFB: https://www.webpagetest.org/.

What is the *right* answer here? What does Google want us to have? Google has recommended that your site have a TTFB of less than 200 ms.

One of the easiest ways to decrease your TTFB is to enable caching on your website. This can help reduce the server processing time.

This brings us to our next step…

#6 Harness the Power of Browser Caching

There's a lot that goes on, on your website. From images to stylesheets, JavaScript files, etc., and as such, can cause a longer load time. By caching your site, the browser doesn't need to reload the entire page each time it's loaded.

If you're using a WordPress website, consider using the W3 Total Cache plugin.

#7 Improve Server Response Time

A Domain Name System (DNS) is a database where all

IP addresses and hostnames are stored. When we type a URL into our browser, our ISP (internet service provider) will perform a DNS lookup to find IP addresses that have been associated with the URL in question. If it takes too much time for your ISP to conduct the DNS lookup, your page speed will be a bit lengthier.

Server response time can be affected by things like:

- Amount of traffic to your website.
- Resources being used on each page.
- The software your server uses.
- Your website's host.

Switching to a faster DNS can speed up the DNS lookup process and ultimately, your page speed.

#8 Optimize and Compress Images

When we say optimization, in this particular instance (improving site speed) we do not mean alt-text (though you shouldn't neglect that either, for other reasons). What we mean by optimization is this:

- Use PNGs for images and/or graphics with 16 colors or less.
- JPGs are better for photographs.

Additionally, you'll want to optimize your images by combining them into CSS sprites (not the drink). CSS image sprites are a collection of images put into a single image. With CSS, you can show just one of the images, not *all* of the images at one time, so no worry there. By combining images into sprites, you can reduce the number of server requests and save some bandwidth. Even if you don't necessarily want to go this route with your images, you should definitely consider it with your buttons and icons.

Image compression is a critical element to improving your site speed. To do this, simply reduce the file size of your images, cropping them to the correct size.

If your website is using WordPress, you can use WP Smush to easily and quickly compress your images. For those not using a WordPress website, there are other tools available such as compressor.io.

#9 Use a Content Distribution Network (CDN)

Content distribution networks can sometimes also be called content delivery networks. They are networks which are used to distribute the load of delivering content. A CDN can help you reduce the load time of your site by caching it on numerous global servers, not just the one you're hosted on.

Without a CDN, when users visit your website, they're all going through your *one* server. Now, if your site is one that drives a fair bit of traffic OR you are planning (because isn't that *everyone's* goal?!) to drive a bunch of traffic to your website, having multiple servers available can help you reduce the load time and we already talked about how people hate waiting. So, that shorter load time is definitely optimal, making a CDN a must!

A great CDN to check out is CloudFlare (https://www.cloudflare.com/).

All right. Let's take a breather because that's a lot to digest. I'll catch you back up here in a few minutes!

Robots.txt Files

Simply put, the robots.txt file is a document that instructs web crawlers/search bots how to crawl the pages on your website. It is essentially a set of rules that say whether certain behaviors of user agents are "allowed" or "disallowed".

A robots.txt file in its most basic for would look like this:

```
User-agent: *
Disallow: /
```

The asterisk after the user agent means that the robots.txt file applies to *all* web robots that visit your website. The slash after disallow tells robots not to visit *any* of your pages.

If you have a lot of pages on your website, it may take the search bots a while to crawl your website, which could then in turn, negatively impact your SEO and ranking. You see, Google has "crawl budget" which identifies how many pages/URLs the search bots (Googlebot in this case) "can and want" to crawl.

If some of your pages contain low quality or duplicate content, those are great pages to consider creating a noindex rule for.

To view your website's current robots.txt file, simply type in your URL/robots.txt and press enter. For example, my website would look like this:

https://www.pendragonconsultingllc.com/robots.txt

This is a very easy way to identify whether you have a

robots.txt file because if you do, then you don't need to create one from scratch.

Creating a Robots.txt File

*Pro-Tip: When creating a robots.txt file, **only use a plain text editor** such as Notepad or TextEdit. Another option is editpad. org (it's free, too!).*

You'll want to go through and locate your robots.txt file. I'd recommend that you copy what's in there and paste it into a new text editor (plain text editor) so that if you make a mistake, you always have the original on hand to start over again.

A basic robots.txt file would look like this:

```
User-agent: *
Disallow:
Sitemap: https://yourURL.com/sitemap.xml
```

In this example, we've said that "rules" will apply to **all** *web robots/search bots*. And by leaving a blank after the "disallow", we've said that everything on our site (all pages) are fair game for the search bots to crawl. Finally, we've also included our sitemap in our robots.txt file (which is recommended - see the next chapter to learn about sitemaps).

*Pro-Tip: robots.txt is case sensitive!!! The file **must** be named robots.txt **NOT** Robots.txt, robots.TXT, etc.*

Technical Robots.txt Syntax

Let me sing to you the language of my people. Well, the language of the robots.txt file is syntax. And here's what you need to know to create your own robots.txt file:

- Allow: This command tells the Google search bots that it is *allowed* to access a page or subfolder.
- Crawl-delay: If you'd like a crawler to wait a couple of seconds before crawling your website, this is where you would set it. Bear in mind that Google does not acknowledge this particular command, and this would only be applicable to other search bots that may be crawling your website.
- Disallow: This particular command tells specific (or all) user-agents *not* to craw particular URL(s). Only *one* disallow line per URL is allowed in your robots. txt file.
- Sitemap: this is used to "callout" the location of your site's XML sitemap. This command is *only* supported by Google, Bing, Ask and Yahoo.
- User-agent: This identifies the specific search bots that your rules or instructions would be applicable to.

*A list of **most** user agents can be accessed here: http://www. robotstxt.org/db.html*

Optimize for SEO

That's right, there's an SEO element here as well - outside of the fact that we're getting our site indexed, of course.

Remember only moments ago when I said that Google has a "crawl budget"? Well, you can optimize for SEO by telling the search bots not to crawl pages that are low quality or duplicate content, for instance. There are a number of other items that could factor in there as well. For example, if your website is built on WordPress, then you'll have a login page that might look like this:

www.yourURL.com/admin

OR

www.yourURL.com/wp-admin

So, let's say we ***don't*** want the search bots to crawl that page. I mean, there's literally no value for SEO on our login page. Our robots.txt file might look like this:

```
User-agent: *
Disallow: /wp-admin/
Allow: /wp-admin/admin-ajax.php
Sitemap: https://yourURL.com/sitemap.xml
```

When you're "disallowing" a page to be crawled, you don't need to include the full URL, but rather, the portion that exists after your .com. So, if your URL looks like this when you login, you will begin immediately following the ".com".:

https://www.yourURL.com/wp-admin/

And it doesn't just stop at your admin pages. For ***any*** page that you don't want crawled, you would simply, again, begin immediately following the ".com".

Testing Your Robots.txt File

Now that you've got your robots.txt file optimized; you'll want to test it. To do this, you'll need to make sure that your website is in Google Search Console. If you're already in there, follow this link to test your robots.txt file:

https://www.google.com/webmasters/tools/robots-testing-tool

If you haven't already setup your GSC, you'll want to get

started on that as we talk about it quite a bit throughout this book. If you click on the link above, you'll see the option to "Add Property Now" so you can get it setup and then test your robots.txt file.

Disclaimer: Your robots.txt file may be ignored by nefarious crawlers, such as malware robots or email address scrapers.

On that note, let's dive into sitemaps.

Creating and Submitting a Sitemap

You'll hear me talking about sitemaps throughout this book, and for good reason. They're how Google and the other search engines learn how to index your website.

Well, let me back pedal a little bit here. If your site is properly linked, the search bots can normally discover most of your site and determine how best to index it (which is a part of why your on-site SEO is so important). However, a sitemap can help you improve the search bots crawling of your site. This is particularly so for those sites that are a bit more complex or specialized.

What Does a Sitemap Do?

A sitemap tells Google the following:

- Which pages and files are important
- When was each page last updated
- How often the pages are updated
- Are there any alternative language versions of the page

Why Do You Need a Sitemap?

Google has come down and laid out the following reasons for why you may need a sitemap:

- Your site is large.
- Your site has a large archive of content pages that are isolated or not well linked to each other.

- Your site is newer and has few external links to it (backlinks).
- Your site has a lot of rich media such as images and video or it's being shown in Google News.

Even if you don't fall under any of those categories, there's no harm in creating one anyways.

How to Build and Submit a Sitemap

There are four different formats that Google will accept your sitemap in:

1. XML
2. RSS, mRSS, and Atom 1.0
3. Text
4. Google Sites

No matter which you choose to use, a single sitemap should not exceed 50MB in its uncompressed form and 50,000 URLs. If you exceed either or both of those, you'll need to break your list down into multiple segments.

You can always build a sitemap by hand, but there are several tools out there that can help generate one for you.

If you're using a WordPress website, you'll want to download the Yoast SEO plugin. In there, you can go into "SEO ◉ General ◉ Features" and then make sure that the "XML sitemaps" is toggled on.

If your website was built in Wix or Squarespace, there's no manual option for editing or controlling your sitemap. Wix allows you to select whether you want the page shown in search engines. If you opt not to have it shown in search engines, this will also add a noindex meta tag to the page in question. Similarly, Squarespace allows you to hide pages from search results with a toggle function.

Submitting a Sitemap

The first step to submitting your sitemap is finding it. Many websites will generate the sitemap for you, and you'll want to find that particular URL. Once you've found it, go into your Google Search Console. On the left side menu, you'll see "Sitemaps". If you click on that, you'll just need to paste the URL you copied from your website into the "Add a new sitemap" bar and hit submit. Easy peasy.

Pro-Tip: In addition to loading your sitemap to GSC, you should also add it to your robots.txt file. To add the sitemap to your robots.txt file, you'll need access to the server. In this instance, you may want to ask a developer or your hosting company for either directions to do it yourself OR for help with getting it loaded in.

Canonicalization

What the what is a canonical tag??? There's soooooo much that goes into SEO, but hopefully by the end of this book you'll feel ready to begin optimizing for Search Engines. The next stop of the SEO train ride is canonicalization, and my friend, this is your stop.

Canonicalization can play an important role in how search engines evaluate the quality of the pages on your website.

If you're putting in some work in releasing an article on a new industry standard or something super important, you may want to have it both on your website AND perhaps, push it out as a press release. The press release holds its own SEO value and can give you some great backlinks, but can you use the same article for both your own website AND the press release? Yes, you can… with canonical tags. In fact, I'd encourage you to do just that. No sense in NOT using the article for both if it's something valuable and important as it could benefit your current and potential customers that you're marketing to in other channels (i.e. blog, social, email).

A canonical tag (also referred to as "rel=canonical") identifies your page as being the original and primary source for that content. This helps to prevent any slaps on the wrist for having duplicate content. Google is not a fan of plagiarism and may downrank your page if it's seen as duplicate content (i.e. potentially plagiarized).

What Does a Canonical Tag Look Like?

Canonical tags use simple syntax and are placed in the

<head> section of your page. A canonical tag would look something like this:

```
<link rel="canonical" href="https://myURL.
com/the-article/" />
```

You can clearly see that's in English but is it?! What in the world does that actually mean??

Link rel="canonical" - this means that this is the master/ original and canonical version of this page.

Href="https://myurl.com/the-article/" - this indicates where the canonical link can be found

Implementing Canonical Tags

There are four main ways to specify your canonical URLs according to Google:

1. Use **rel="canonical"** link tag

2. Use **rel="canonical"** HTTP header

3. Use a sitemap

4. Use 301 redirects for retired URLs

Before we dive into how to implement those for the four different ways, here's what you need to know.

*Use **absolute** paths rather than relative paths with the rel="canonical" link element. This applies to both #1 and #2 - link tag AND HTTP header.*

What that means is that you need to spell out the entire URL: https://www.myURL.com/the-article/ and NOT just /the-article/.

#1 Link Tag

In the <head> section of your page, you want to mark duplicate pages with the rel="canonical" link tag by doing the following (obviously, you'll need to use your own URL in place of my example one):

```
<link rel="canonical" href="https://www.
yourURL.com/the-article/" />
```

#2 HTTP Header

Rather than add an HTML tag, you can include the canonical URL for non-HTML documents, such as PDFs. There may be times in which you will be linking directly to a .PDF that will open in a tab, showing a URL and everything. Here's how you would add the rel=canonical link:

```
Link: https://www.yourURL.com/downloads/the-
article.pdf; rel="canonical"
```

#3 Sitemap

This one is perhaps the easiest and least reliable way. By ensuring the link is included on your sitemap, it will indicate that *all* of those links included are canonical. The Google search bots will determine which, if any, pages are duplicates.

Now, it's important to note that they've clearly provided a disclaimer saying that they do not guarantee that they'll consider sitemap URLs to be canonical.

For pages that are *NOT* canonical - meaning you're not the original owner - you shouldn't include them on your sitemap. Don't waste Google's "crawl budget" by including non-canonical links.

#4 301 Redirects for Retired URLs

If you've had your website for a number of years, you may have some retired URLs, such as:

https://yourURL.com/home

https://www.yourURL.com

https://home.yourURL.com

You'll see this come up again in our SEO Audit at the end of the book.

From here, you'll want to ensure that only ONE of your pages goes to the homepage, and not all three of those. You can set up 301 redirects to direct the user to the ONE page you've selected.

This is mainly for duplicate pages/variants of getting to your page and not necessarily to our article and press release example.

What Canonicalization Is NOT

There are those that are misinformed, and I'd like to quickly clear up some of those items:

1. Canonicalization is NOT a redirect.

2. It is NOT a directive. (A directive is something that the search engines will automatically follow.)

3. Canonicalization IS a signal, which serves as a *hint* for search engines, which may then *choose* whether or not to use.

Canonical Tags v. 301 Redirects

As mentioned above, one of the primary misconceptions about what canonicalization is and what it is not is that some users tend to believe that canonicalization is the same as a redirect. It is not.

Let's take a look at both and how they function.

301 Redirect

Sally came across a link she wants to visit. That page no longer exists, so she's been redirected - *unbeknownst to her* - to a similar page. Sally was never shown the website she initially intended to visit, but rather *only* the page that she was redirected to.

Canonical Tag

In this instance, we'll say that www.yourURL.com has the same article on it that www.myURL.com has and we've set up the rel=canonical link indicating that the link to www.myURL.com was the original source of content. Sally - and all other users - will still be able to visit BOTH websites.

Auditing Your Canonical Tags

You can find the answer to this question by right-clicking on the page in question and clicking on "View Page Source".

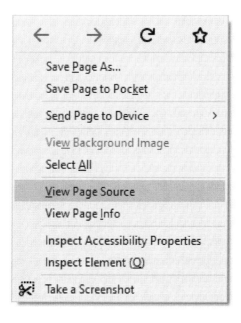

From here, you're looking for the <head> tag and then, the <link rel="canonical"... tag - if one has been created for the page in question.

```
1   <!DOCTYPE html>
2   <html lang="en">
3   <head>
4
5     <meta charset='utf-8'>
6     <meta name="viewport" content="
7     <meta http-equiv="X-UA-Compatib
8     <base href="https://www.pendrag
9     <meta name="generator" content=
10
11    <link rel="icon" sizes="192x192
12    <link rel="shortcut icon" href=
13    <link rel="apple-touch-icon" hr
14    <!-- Safari Pinned Tab Icon -->
15    <!-- <link rel="mask-icon" href
16
```

You can see from my example here that the number 1 starts at the top of the page, so the <head> tag is right there, near the top, as it should be. Not much farther down, you'll see the link tags. Now, I do not have an example in this image, BUT if this page *did* have a rel="canonical" tag, that is where it would appear.

You can also run audits in places like Moz, SEMRush or Ahrefs as well to see if you're missing any canonical tags.

When auditing your canonical tags for SEO, there are three things you'll want to be looking for:

1. Does the page have a canonical tag?

2. Does the tag point to the correct page?

3. Are they crawlable and indexable?

Common Mistakes to Avoid

Mistakes happen. That's why we have a list here of some of the most common ones because *many* people have made these mistakes. Use these to your advantage and avoid following in their footsteps!

- Don't block the canonical link in your robots.txt file.
- Do not set your canonical URL to "noindex".
- Do use hreflang tags with canonical tags.
- Do not use multiple canonical tags.
- Do put your canonical link in the <head> and NOT in the <body>.

Hreflang

Yup. You read it right - or did you?! Is it an offshoot of "wu tang" (like wu tang clan) pronunciation? Lord knows when I first started with SEO, I sure did have to watch a YouTube video to figure out how to pronounce this bad boy.

Hreflang is yet another tag for your website. Here's where they differ, though.

The purpose of hreflang tags is to provide a way to mark up your pages that are similar, but that provide content in different languages and/or regions. Let's say that our website provides services to America, Great Britain and Australia and we have similar pages on our website targeting those specific regions. We could use the hreflang tag to tell Google that they're similar and this is why so that we don't get knocked for duplicate content.

If you are a company offering international services, you may want to consider having multiple pages set up that are similar, but that offer it in language and/or regional variables.

Again, if I'm offering services to the United States, the United Kingdom and Australia, then I probably also want to make sure that I'm ranking in those three regions, using their natural spelling/dialect (color v. colour, for instance). To do this, you can create multiple variants of your page and then tag them with the hreflang tag to make that known.

Remember, it all comes down to the user experience for those querying search engines like Google. If they're in

Australia, but my pages are all in the U.S. (en-us), then chances are pretty high I'm not going to rank in Australia. By having that similar page with the hreflang tag, it says to Google okay, their site is hitting all the right elements in the ranking algorithm AND they're located in the right region, so they'll decide to show your results more.

Implementing hreflang Tags

Just like canonical links, hreflangs also have three of the same ways as canonical links to implement these tags:

1. HTML hreflang in <head>
2. Hreflang HTTP header
3. Sitemap

#1 HTML hreflang in <head>

Each variation of your page should link to every other variation. If your site is larger, this option may not be your best avenue of approach as it can get lengthy and slow your load time down.

```
<link rel="alternate" href="https://myURL.
com/" hrefland="en" />
<link rel="alternate" href="https://myURL.
com/" hrefland="en-gb" />
<link rel="alternate" href="https://myURL.
com/" hrefland="en-au" />
```

#2 HTTP Header

The HTTP header is again, for PDF and other non-HTML content. They would look like this:

```
Link: https://www.myURL.com/document.pdf;
rel="alternate"; hreflang="en"
```

```
Link: https://www.myURL.com/document.pdf;
rel="alternate"; hreflang="es"
Link: https://www.myURL.com/document.pdf;
rel="alternate"; hreflang="de"
```

#3 Sitemap

We've already covered how to create and edit your sitemap. To implement your hreflang tags in your sitemap, it would look like this:

```
<url>
   <loc>http://www.myURL.com/uk/</loc>
   <xhtml:link rel="alternate" hreflang="en"
href="http://www.myURL.com/" />
   <xhtml:link rel="alternate" hreflang="en-
au" href="http://www.myURL.com/au/" />
   <xhtml:link rel="alternate" hreflang="en-
gb" href="http://www.myURL.com/uk/" />
</url>
```

In the sitemap implementation, this is the easiest way to implement your hreflangs as implementing this on your site may be quite a bit more complicated.

To help you with your hreflang tags, Aleyda Solis has created a hreflang tag generator tool which makes this process that much easier:

https://www.aleydasolis.com/english/international-seo-tools/hreflang-tags-generator/

Finding and Fixing Broken Links

Visiting a broken link is a total downer. Wine and dine your website visitors by providing an optimal user experience. Not only will broken links harm your UX, but it can also negatively impact your SEO - again, another big item here that will be *even more* of a factor when Google rolls out their Page Experience update.

If a user stumbles on a broken link, what happens? They move on to the next search result and don't look back. You've just lost them. Even if they wanted to, a broken link doesn't contain any other links to your site, they literally can't see any other links to stay on your site. Bam. They've moved on and that could have been a potential customer, so you've now lost money.

Broken links are links to URLs that no longer exist, which will subsequently trigger a 404-error page.

How to Check for Broken Links on Your Website

Let's not pretend there's only one way to do this…

There's a tool called Broken Link Checker in which you can check for broken links *for free* by visiting their website at: https://www.brokenlinkcheck.com/. They also have a free Google Chrome extension that you can get for your browser to check for broken links on the fly.

If you're wondering how often you should check for broken links, I'd recommend once a month to once a quarter unless you have a larger site in which case once a week to once a month.

Fixing Broken Links

This should be obvious here, but I'll dive in anyways.

To fix a broken link, you'll want to either create a redirect if it's one of your own pages that no longer exist *and also* update the link to the new, similar one on your website OR if it's a link to an external page (not your website, but rather someone else's site) you can simply replace the link with another comparable link.

Find and Fix Crawl Errors

If you're looking at crawl errors, that means that you're in Google Search Console - and rightly so. That is where we'll be working for this chapter.

What is crawling?

Before we can answer what a crawl error is, we'll start by looking at what *crawling* is. Crawling is the process of search bots visiting each page of your website to learn what each page is about, to index them and to determine how to rank them.

What is a crawl error?

A crawl error is when search bots (such as the Googlebots) try to crawl your website but fail for whatever reason.

How do you know if there are any crawl errors on your website?

To find out if there are any crawl errors on your website, visit your Google Search Console and check out the "Coverage" tab on the left-side menu. It gives you a 90 day overview of any crawl errors that may have occurred.

How do you fix crawl errors in Google Search Console?

If your site does have crawl issues, the exact issues will appear in the Coverage report. On that same page, if you scroll down a bit, you'll see "Details". In there, Google tells you specifically what the errors are. You can then click on the specific error to learn more about the issue(s). This gives you at least some information that you can use to determine the best course of action. Once you've successfully corrected the error, you can then go back into your Google Search Console to validate that you've fixed the error and ask Google to re-crawl your page.

Do not ignore crawl errors as they can take your rankings from bad to worse.

How often should you check for crawl errors in GSC?

You should strive to check for crawl errors in GSC weekly. If you are not updating your site very often, you could probably get away with monthly. The caveat here is that the longer that goes between you checking for crawl errors, the longer you may face issues. Some issues may have catastrophic impact on your site and your rankings, so bear that in mind as you move forward with your SEO strategy.

If you aim for every 90 days *at a minimum*, you can see any issues you may have had in the last 90 days and can help you shape your way forward. If you had a URL issue during the 90 day period that resolved itself, you may face that issue again in the future so going back through and fixing it would be the best way forward.

Types of Crawl Errors

Now that you have a basic understanding of how to find and fix crawl errors, let's get a bit more technical and look at the various types of crawl errors. There are two main areas that GSC will divide errors into:

1. Site Issues
2. URL Issues

Site issues are considered to be "high-level" issues and could negatively impact your website, so make sure to resolve these issues in a timely manner. Issues of this nature can impact your usability, which can be *catastrophic* to your website's ability to function *and* to rank. Remember that Google places special emphasis on the user experience and if your site isn't functioning, that's pretty central to the heart of the user experience. They're not going to show your site in the Search results if your site isn't working. Their focus is on the UX and if you're not able to deliver that, you simply won't rank.

URL issues are not as catastrophic as they relate to a single page and not the overall site. While less urgent, URL issues should be resolved when you can and should not be ignored.

In each of those categories (site and URL), there are a number of various issues that you could face. Let's dive in a bit deeper here....

1. Site issues
    1. DNS errors
    2. Server errors
    3. Robots failure
2. URL errors
    1. Soft 404
    2. 404
    3. Access denied
    4. Not followed
    5. Server errors & DNS errors

DNS Errors

DNS stands for Domain Name Server and if there is a crawl error relating to the DNS, it means that Google has either faced a timeout issue OR a lookup issue. Either way, the way to fix these would be to work with your domain provider as this error means the bots can't *find* your website.

Let's say that your website is built on WordPress. WordPress is **not** where you would have purchased your domain. You likely purchased it through another vendor such as GoDaddy, Namecheap or somewhere else.

To find out if your website is down for you *or for everyone*, you can visit this URL to check for free: https://downforeveryoneorjustme.com/

Server Errors

The most common form of a *server error* is that the server is taking too long to respond to the Google Search bots. If it takes too long, the bots will simply give up and move on. So, while a DNS error means that the bots can't find your website, a server error means that they can find your site, but that the page/site won't load.

Like a DNS error, a server error is detrimental to Google's ability to crawl your site. This error can have catastrophic ramifications.

To determine whether your site is still facing server errors in GSC, simply input the URL in the URL inspection tool in your GSC. If the error shows as resolved, great, but you'll still want to investigate to see what the specific issue was to prevent it from happening again in the future.

Here are some common server issues:

- Timeout
- Truncated Headers
- Connection Reset
- Truncated Response
- Connection Refused
- Connect Failed
- Connect Timeout
- No Response

Google Search Console can provide some excellent information on how to resolve those specific issues. You can also reach out your webmaster for assistance in fixing those particular errors as well.

Robots Failure

A robots failure refers to Google Search bots not being able to retrieve your robots.txt file.

Again, you can find your robots.txt file by typing in:

www.**yoursiteURL**.com/robots.txt

The robots.txt file is important if there are pages on your site *that you do **not** want Google to crawl*. To fix this issue, it's as easy as checking to see if you have a robots.txt file and if you do, is it accurate. If you don't have a robots.txt file, you'll want to consider if you need one. If Google is allowed to crawl all pages on your site, then you likely don't need a robots.txt file.

Soft 404

A soft 404 issue is when a page returns a 200 code rather than a 404. The HTTP header response code should be a

404 (not found) or a 410 (gone baby, gone).

Another point of contention here would be if you have a 301 redirect setup for a page that no longer exists redirecting a page that *is not relevant* to the original page.

So, the fix would be to ensure that 1) your HTTP header is using the appropriate code and 2) you are using 301 redirects to send traffic to *related* pages and not your homepage or other unrelated page.

404

A 404 error means that the Google Search bots attempted to crawl a page on your website that does not exist. While Google has gone on to say that 404 issues do not affect your ranking, they do affect your user and page experience which ***does*** ultimately affect your ranking in a roundabout way. So, it's best <u>not</u> to ignore these issues, especially as the "fix" is a fairly simple solution.

There are two ways to resolve this issue... you can either reinstate the page or create a 301 redirect to redirect any search traffic (and the bots) to another ***relevant*** page.

Access Denied

Just as it sounds, Google's Search bots are ***not*** able to access or crawl your page. An "access denied" error can stem from a number of reasons. For instance, if you've created a members only area on your site that users must login to, Google will not be able to access your page. Similarly, if you've disallowed access on your robots.txt file, Google will not have access to crawling that page.

If either of these apply to you, you may want to have a

quick peek at your robots.txt file to ensure that Google has access to all of the pages that it should have access to as this *could* impact your rankings.

Not Followed

These are not the same as "nofollow". This means that Google was not able to follow the URL. Google may have issues crawling the following:

• JavaScript
• Cookies
• Session IDs
• Frames
• DHTML
• Flash

To view your page/site as the Googlebots would view it as they crawl it, you can download a Google Chrome extension called "<u>User-Agent-Switcher</u>". If the pages aren't loading while you're using the Chrome extension due to one of the items on the list above, you've solved your problem.

Server & DNS Errors

All right. I know we've talked about this one under "Site Errors", but Google also lists it under the "URL Errors" as well. They would appear under URL as opposed to Site if this was only applicable to a particular page and not the site as a whole.

Google has commented saying that to resolve this issue for Server & DNS errors under the URL Errors, the same process used for Site Errors should be used to resolve those under URL errors.

To learn more, check out Google's <u>Webmaster Search Central Help Community</u>

(<u>https://support.google.com/webmasters/community/?hl=en&gpf=%23!forum%2Fwebmasters</u>).

One tool in particular to assist with this process is Screaming Frog SEO Spider (<u>https://www.screamingfrog.co.uk/seo-spider/</u>). In fact, this tool can help you with quite a number of SEO related tasks.

You can also run a Site Audit using your SEMrush *free trial* to further suss out your crawl and SEO errors.

Creating an SEO Friendly URL Structure

In this chapter we will discuss some practices which you can employ to create an SEO friendly URL structure for your website. We'll also cover why this is important and what the benefits of employing these practices are.

Prior to diving into structure, let's first break down URLs to give you a better understanding of what we're talking about.

What Is a URL?

A Uniform Resource Locator (URL) is what specifies the location of an internet resource. It will specify to your browser how to retrieve it and where to find it. URLs are human readable texts used to replace the IP addresses computers use to communicate.

They consist of a protocol, domain name, top-level domain (TLD) and path with a format that looks like this:

protocol://domain-name.top-level-domain/path

- **Protocol:**
  Protocol tells the browser what protocol to follow to retrieve the information from the resource.
- **Domain name:**
  Domain name is a human-readable name of the location of the resource, which in most cases is a website.
- **Top-level domain (TLD):**
  TLD is the category of website you are trying to

access like, '.com', '.edu' or '.org'.
- **Path:**
  Path includes the specific subfolder structure where a page on the website is located.

Now that you understand URLs better, let's look at SEO friendly URLs.

What Is an SEO Friendly URL?

An SEO friendly URL is a URL that is optimized for SEO. It meets the needs of the users, searchers and search engines. They present your URL in such a way that it is easy for both humans and search engines to read and understand. They are typically short and tend to be keyword rich.

Why Use SEO Friendly URLs?

The main reasons to use SEO friendly URLs is to drive more traffic to your website and improve rankings in search results. Using SEO friendly URLs, you can clearly state to the users and the search engines what the contents of your page are.

Search engines can better understand the contents if they can correctly read the URL, this makes it easier for them to refer users to it. Users have a better experience because SEO friendly URLs make it easier for them to read and understand the contents as well.

Another benefit is that a well-written and easily understandable URL provides a better user experience when you link your URL to blogs, social media platforms or any other online outlet.

Creating an SEO Friendly URL Structure

When creating an SEO friendly URL, you want to structure the URL in such a way that it ranks higher, is user friendly and will bring the relevant users to your page. Here are a few key things to practice.

Structure Your URLs

Creating a site-wide structure for your website is important if you want to future-proof your website and URLs. It is always a good idea to categorize your website, so you know what goes where. Doing this will make for a better user experience and will also help organize your URLs in the future.

You want the path of your URL to reflect the hierarchy of your website. It should read in a flow that looks like 'domain-category-subcategory-page'. Using a clear hierarchy with a logical folder structure in URLs will not only help users but will also help search engines better understand how you categorize your website. It is also better to keep fewer folders to reduce depth perception of your website in users and search engines, although this is not always necessary. You should judge this according to your website.

Incorporate Keywords

When adding a page on your domain(website), it is important to have a clear vision of what the purpose and contents of the page are. Once you have an understanding of the page's content, you can incorporate the right keywords in its URL that are relevant to the content. You can perform keyword research to see which keywords suit the content better.

Incorporating keywords on your page's URL will allow search engines to easily understand the contents and display your URL to relevant search queries. This will help bring the right people to your page.

Use Hyphens to Separate Words

Using hyphens, or even underscores, is a great way to separate words in your URL to make it easier for users to read. Increased readability will allow for a better and more friendly user experience.

Easy to Read URL

Along with your URLs being keyword rich, it is also important to simultaneously make sure that the URL is easy-to-read. You want to keep your URLs simple, relevant and as accurate as possible. This makes it easier to incorporate the right keywords and maintain a user-friendly experience.

The URL should allow users and search engines to have a good idea of what the page is about by simply reading its URL.

Use Shorter URLs

Shorter URLs are usually better than longer ones. If your page's URL is around sixty characters, then you do not have to worry about its length. But if it is a hundred characters or longer, then you might want to think about cutting it short.

Keeping the URLs short does not make a difference to search engines, this is so that the users have a better experience while reading the URL. You want them to understand the content in as few words as possible and grab their attention in as little time as possible.

Shorter URLs are also easier to share. They do not take too much space when being shared on social media platforms, especially on platforms like Twitter where they have limited character space.

Canonicalize URLs

If you have two or more URLs that have very similar content, you might want to prioritize one over the other or consider canonicalizing them. You can use a 301 redirect if you want users to get redirected to the more relevant or updated page of the two.

Similarly, if you want to keep both pages, you can use a rel=canonical to maintain both different versions. It is important to canonicalize URLs because duplicate content can cause a split of ranking signals that damage your search traffic potential. By canonicalizing the pages, you can create a better opportunity for the more important page to rank and gain traffic.

These are just some of the ways to improve the structure of your URLs to make them SEO friendly and allow for a better user experience. A single line of characters that we call URLs can have a big impact on your website. If you structure URLs correctly, it can benefit you, the users and the search engines simultaneously.

There are many other things you can practice while structuring your URLs and it is always a good idea to keep learning to improve your website and traffic.

Understanding Structured Data

Here's another chapter that may cause you some indigestion... In this chapter we'll discuss structured data - what it is, how it is used and why you should be using it. This chapter will hopefully provide you with a basic understanding of the way structured data helps drive organic traffic to your business or website.

What Is Structured Data?

Structured Data is simply Information that is organized in such a way that it is easy for Google (and the other search engines) to read. Structured data allows Google to understand the information on a webpage to make it possible for it to be displayed as a rich result in Google searches.

Simply put, it is 'data' that is 'structured' for Google.

Although not exclusively for Google, structured data can be used for any search engine. It communicates the contents (data) of a webpage to search engines in an organized (structured) manner.

Similar to a markup language like HTML or XML, structured data is a markup language. It helps define elements within a document, which in this case, is your webpage.

The contents of structured data are not visible to webpage visitors, they are only seen by search engines. It enables search engines to identify and label things like specific images, names, ratings and details of items or elements on your webpage.

Using structured data, search engines do not have to rely on complicated algorithms to define a product or image in your webpage. Structured data defines and labels these things for the search engine to identify.

Communicating this data to search engines requires a vocabulary just like any form of communication. In the case of big search engines like Google, this vocabulary is Schema.org.

What Does Schema.org Do?

Schema.org is a joint effort of big search engines to organize and code the information on your webpage. It is the official website used by Google for structured data.

Schema.org has a large collection of codes that translate structured data to Google. The codes allow you to organize the contents of your webpage in a way that is readable by Google. You will find all the structured data markup supported by Google on Schema.org.

You can use these codes on your webpage for Google to understand what the contents of your webpage are and how to best present them in searches.

If, for example, you are selling a product on your webpage, Schema.org codes can define and outline the details of your product to Google through codes.

This allows Google to understand your product and display it as rich results in Google searches.

How Is Structured Data Used

Google has used structured data for a long time.

As time progressed, Google updated how and where it used the structured data from your webpage. The main platform for structured data is 'Rich Results' or 'Rich Snippets'.

A rich result appears at the top of the results page, often in the coveted "position zero", above traditional text results, in the form of a snippet. These snippets are search results that are richer than normal snippets.

A normal snippet will show the title, meta description and URL of your webpage, whereas a rich snippet will show these and add more eye-catching and informative details.

These rich snippets include:

- **Paragraph Snippets**
  Text from a webpage to answer a search query that usually starts with 'why', 'what' or 'who'.
- **Numbered List Snippets**
  Step-by-step list to execute a specific task for a search query usually starting with 'how'.
- **Bulleted List Snippets**
  Numbered snippets replaced by bullets, usually to display listicles.
- **Table Snippets**
  Represent data from a webpage relevant to the search query in table format.
- **YouTube Snippets**
  Display a section of a YouTube video optimized for a specific query.

Rich snippets are the best form of results on Google

searches and they are optimized on your webpage through structured data.

If your webpage qualifies for a rich result, then search engines like Google may choose to display your content as a rich snippet.

Why Use Structured Data?

The reason for structured data is simple. More traffic.

You will be able to display your product or service in an attractive and informative way on Google's search results to increase Click Through Rate (CTR).

All the small details of the rich snippets mentioned above are possible because the webpage used structured data to optimize their content.

Detailed rich results present a more inviting prospect for users to click through to your site and search engine algorithms recognize high CTRs, often boosting rankings for your website.

You can utilize structured data to increase organic traffic to your webpage. This will help you expand your business to a larger audience.

If your rich result makes it to the top of Google's results page, it will also enable voice searches to feature your rich snippet to users who use voice searches.

Because voice searches dictate the results, your content will be the first to be heard by users who are otherwise occupied in tasks and cannot physically search on the internet.

301 & 302 Redirects

By this point you should at least be a little familiar with 301 redirects. If you're still a little iffy on it, don't worry, we'll go into it a bit more in this chapter.

What are redirects?

Redirects are ways of redirecting both uses and Searchbots away from a particular page to a new page. A redirect should send traffic to a relevant page to the topic of the original page.

For instance, if we are redirecting traffic from a page discussing an apple pie recipe, we would want to *redirect* the traffic to a page also discussing an apple pie recipe.

If you redirect to a page that is not relevant to the topic of the original page, you'll experience a higher bounce rate and Google may see this as a poor-quality page. Hence the importance of relevancy when redirecting traffic.

Types of Redirects

There are three types of redirects out there:

1. 301 Redirect
2. 302 Redirect
3. Meta Refresh

301 Redirect

A 301 redirect is most commonly used for SEO as it tells both users and the search bots that the page has _**permanently**_ moved. In this instance, permanent means a year or longer.

You might consider a 301 redirect if you've acquired a new URL and don't want to lose those who are looking for your old website. You can also use 301 redirects to direct users to your site based on common misspellings. Here's another common time in which you'd want to set up your 301 redirect.

Your website can be found as:

www.yourURL.com

https://yourURL.com

https://www.yourURL.com

Those are three different ways you can get to your website. Now, if you type all three of those into your site and look at the browser bar, do they automatically redirect to a particular URL?

For instance, my own URL is https://www. pendragonconsultingllc.com. However, if we were to type in https://pendragonconsultingllc.com, it would redirect to https://www.pendragonconsultingllc.com. You'll even find links in all of my books that are sent to www. pendragonconsultingllc.com that will all take you to my beautiful website with the prime URL. That's because my 301 redirects are set up that way.

If you find that when you type in the browser the variations of your URL, you'll want to go in there and set up your own 301 redirects for it.

302 Redirects

A 302 redirect functions the same as a 301 redirect with one exception: a 301 redirect is ***permanent,*** and a 302 redirect is ***temporary***.

While 301 redirects will be the primary redirect most will end up using, a temporary redirect (302) is good for when you're diverting traffic *temporarily* while you're redesigning your website.

How to Set Up Redirects

Many CMS platforms such as Wix and WordPress have simplified the process through the use of their in-house tools (Wix) or Plugins that you can download (WordPress). Both allow you to go in there and tinker with the code, but if you're not sure what you're doing, that may not be the best option.

Some WordPress plugin options are:

• "Redirection"
• "SEO Redirection"
• "Simple 301 Redirects"

Whichever redirect you end up using, be sure to keep an eye on your Search engine rankings to ensure that your redirects have not caused any issues.

Part IV

The Extra Bits

Google Search Console

If you've made any changes or updates to your website, such as to your web copy, your structure, even adding a blog, you'll want to request Google to re-index your website, or the new page you've just updated or added and not necessarily the whole website (unless you've just built or completely redone your website). Without making this request, it can take a few weeks or even months before Google's bots crawl your website to re-index it on its own.

Google has bots that crawl every page out there on the internet in order to gather information and organize it in the Search index.

Let's simplify this a bit for those not familiar with this topic. If your website is not indexed by Google/Google's bots, it will not appear in Google's search results. If you're trying to maximize your exposure or to rank for specific keywords, you can see where the problem lies.

Do you remember our chapter on heading tags? One of the things we mentioned was that for Google (and the other search engines) to understand your website and how to index it (or classify it), you need to use your heading tags on your website appropriately - otherwise when the bots crawl your website they will leave confused and not rank you as well as you might otherwise be able to rank.

Three Steps to Indexing Your Website's Content

This is just a broad overview of the steps. If you get hung up on verifying ownership of your website with Google

Search Console, there are loads of videos out there on YouTube that can help walk you through step by step what you need to do. Of course, if you're working with a marketing agency or a website developer, they can assist you with this process as well.

Set Up Google Search Console

The first step to requesting that Google re-index your website is by setting up your Google Search Console. This means connecting your website with Google Search Console. Here's what you'll need to do:

Click on the three lines in the top left corner and select "+ Add Property".

You'll be prompted to select either Domain or URL Prefix. The choice is yours, but URL prefix may be easier to setup if you're doing it on your own. From here, you'll be able to select how to verify ownership of the website/ URL. Some of those options include through HTML tag in which you'd upload the HTML file to your website, if you've already setup Google Analytics or Google Tag

Manager on your website, those are also ways in which you can verify your site ownership.

Conduct a URL Inspection

Once you've verified ownership, you can check out your dashboard for a quick snapshot look at what's going on with your website.

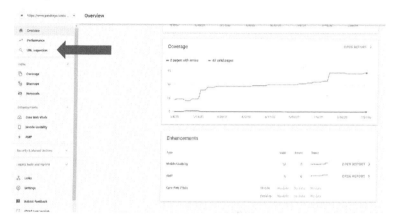

If you're not sure whether your page is indexed with Google, there are one of two ways in which you can verify that it is. The first, through Google Search Console since we're already here, is to click on the tab called "URL inspection" from the left side menu. This will highlight the search bar at the top of the screen. Enter your URL in there to check whether the page has been indexed.

It may take a few minutes to retrieve results. If the page has been indexed, you'll get a screen that looks like this:

The second way of checking to see if your website has been indexed by Google is to type into a Google search bar:

Site: www.yourwebsite.com/pageyouwanttocheck

Obviously, that URL should be the URL you're looking to inspect. You do not have to "own" this URL to see it through this method. However, to request indexing, you do need to own it. So, head back over to Google Search Console and let's get your page indexed/re-indexed.

Request Indexing/Re-Indexing

Let's say that you've refreshed your older content to make

it more relevant and timelier, or even updated one of your main pages. If that is the case, you'll want to request that Google re-index your website. To accomplish this, you'll want to click on "Request Indexing". It may take a few hours to days for Google to crawl your updated content. You don't need to click on it more than once, just try to have some patience with it and if it's not re-indexed by the end of the week, you can always try again.

To determine whether the Google bots have crawled your website recently, simply expand the "Coverage" tab and it will tell you the date and time the page was crawled along with the type of bot. The type of bot is important and will more often than not be a form of mobile bot as more and more users spend the majority of their time online through mobile devices. Always make sure your website and the content are mobile optimized to avoid any penalties.

If the page is not yet on Google, you'll get a screen that looks like this:

URL Inspection

All you have to do is click on "Request Indexing" and let the magic happen. Well, maybe not magic, but you do have to have patience while the bots queue up to crawl your website.

As you continue to index your content with website and begin a routine pace of posting new content, Google and it's bots will learn the frequency and begin to crawl your website at more frequent intervals to keep up with your pace of fresh content.

Websites such as The New York Times produces content all day long. A financial planner may only update their website with a new blog once a month. Google will crawl The New York Times fairly rapidly whereas the financial planner's website may only get crawled once every few weeks - or less.

And that's that. Always make sure your content is indexed. Otherwise, all that work may be for nothing - at least until the bots learn of its existence. However, if you're going to do the work, why not make sure you get the best ROI you can get from it, especially if that means you'll be able to rank higher on Google (or the other search engines).

Setting Up Google Analytics

If you haven't already installed Google Analytics on your website, I'd encourage you to do so. By installing this on your website, you can view:

- Bounce Rate
- Number of visitors
- Time and Day of the week users are most active on your website
- Which pages are most popular and which could use some improvement
- Who is vising your website
- How are they browsing your website
- How are they finding you/where are they coming from (referral traffic)
- Where are they located (demographics)
- Are they using mobile devices or a desktop
- Bonus: Connect to your Google Ads to see the conversion rate

There are many reasons why Google Analytics is awesome, and you need to have it. Did you know that it's free?!

If you want a better feel for your Return on Investment, install GA to track and measure your website's traffic. Installing it and understanding it may look intimidating, but it is so worth it and there are a ton of YouTube videos out there that can help walk you through how to set up Google Analytics on your specific website (Wix, WordPress, Weebly, etc.).

To install Google Analytics on your website, you'll need to have administrative access to the website and be able to place the tracking ID on your site. Some sites, like Wix, have made it super easy to place the tracking ID on your site, even WordPress has

Once you've got your Google Analytics set up on your website, you can also link directly from your Google Analytics account to your Google Ads account AND Google Search Console, making using the Google suite of tools even easier and that much more streamlined.

Running an SEO Audit

We've talked a lot about SEO by this point. What happens if you've taken all of this into account and applied it to your own website, but you're still not seeing the results you'd like? Or perhaps, your competitors are still outranking you despite your best efforts. If that's the case, you may want to perform an SEO audit.

But where to start....

What is an SEO Audit?

By definition, an SEO audit is an audit of your website's SEO and is the process of identifying issues that could prevent your website from ranking higher on Google or the other search engines. Remember that the higher you rank, the more traffic your website would get and ultimately, more traffic means more sales.

Reasons to Consider a SEO Audit

1. You've experienced a drop in *organic* traffic.
   Always check to see if there was an algorithm update that could be wreaking havoc on your SEO.

2. You just bought a website, and you'd like to determine which your next steps should be.

3. You're awesome enough to recognize the necessity for periodic reviews of your website's SEO. Consider quarterly to semi-annual checks.

4. You just started working in a marketing role for a company - never make assumptions that you're coming into an optimized website.

Tools Required for Running an SEO Audit

- Google Analytics
- Google Search Console
- Google PageSpeed Insights
- Google's Structured Data Testing Tool
- Web Page Word Counter
- Copyscape
- Ahrefs OR SemRush (both offer a free trial)
- Majestic

Can I just take a second to tell you that while all of these tools are effective and awesome, I have a particular fondness for Majestic (https://majestic.com). You want to dig deep and look at your backlinks to make sure that you don't have any poor quality or spammy links to keep your SEO top tier? This is THE tool. It gives you a complete deep look at your links from who is linking to you, trust flow, density, languages and anchor text to name a few.

How To Run An SEO Audit

Buckle up because we're about to get technical (and super nerdy). Seriously, I hope you paid attention through the book because in a way, this will be a test of your newly discovered knowledge.

Step 1: SEMRush Site Audit

Take a deep breath.

Now, to get your whereabouts and find some good direction, let's first start by running your website through a tool such as SEMRush's Site Audit tool. SEMRush allows you ONE free project, so make the most of it! However, like Ahref's if that's the direction you choose to go, SEMRush offers a 7 day free trial.

Once you've started your free trial, go ahead and click on "new site audit" at the top right. Outside of entering your website/URL, you shouldn't need to adjust any settings.

Step 2: Check for Duplicate Versions

While you're waiting for this to generate, go ahead and check to ensure that only one version of your website is browsable. If multiple versions of your site are indexed, you'll want to correct that asap. What we mean by that is this:

www.pendragonconsultingllc.com

https://www.pendragonconsultingllc.com

https://pendragonconsultingllc.com

You see how we have three versions there? If you click on any of them it should redirect to ONE of those. In the case of my website, the second one there is where the other two redirect to. If you click on each version of your website and find that you can find your website by all THREE (or however many), you'll want to set up your 301 redirects to the canonical version of your website.

Pro tip: Ensure that your website is using HTTPS and not HTTP as Google and the other search engines will give you a slight ranking boost over HTTP websites for SSL enabled sites. Having an HTTPS website also means that your website is more secure, which in and of itself is a plus, but it also helps to ensure that those browsing your website can trust your site.

Another way to check for duplicate versions of your site is if you head to Google and type in the search bar: "site:YOURURL". For example, mine would look like this: "site:pendragonconsultingllc.com".

By querying Google for that search strand, you can see all of the URLs that have been indexed by Google. If a page is missing, that may indicate that your page has not been crawled/indexed by Google, in which case, you can request indexing through your Google Search Console account.

Step 3: Google Search Console & Manual Actions

Ensure your website is verified in Google Search Console.

Now, you'll need to go through a verification process to essentially prove to Google that you in fact own the website in question. If you get stuck on this, there are loads of YouTube videos that can help walk you through the specific process for your site (i.e. WordPress, Wix, Weebly, etc.).

One of the biggest things you'll want to check for in Google Search Console is "manual actions". If your site has been deemed to be in violation of <u>Google's Webmaster Quality Guidelines</u>, you'll be given a slap on the wrist and they'll issue a manual action.

Manual actions can and will impact your website's ranking ability until the action is revoked. In fact, Google has the ability to deindex your entire site, meaning you won't even rank for the name of your brand/company.

Step 4: Page Speed

The next stop on our tour of SEO audits takes us to checking your website's speed. While I enjoy a good bit of humor here and there, I'm not actually kidding about this. The faster your website, the better off you'll fare. Slower loading times can actually harm your SEO and rankings.

Pay particular attention to this section… Google has announced in 2020 that they would be rolling out a new algorithm update in 2021 called Page Experience. This means that you have some time to ensure that your website provides an optimal page/user experience (UX) for your website viewers. Once this update rolls out, many, many sites will find that they are no longer ranking as well as they were for this very reason.

Google actually released data showing that the longer it takes your website to load, the more likely you'll see an increase in the bounce rate. Check it out here:

https://www.thinkwithgoogle.com/marketing-strategies/app-and-mobile/mobile-page-speed-new-industry-benchmarks/

To check your website's speed, follow this link (totally free):

https://developers.google.com/speed/pagespeed/insights/

Step 5: Check Mobile Friendliness

It's a mobile-first world, ladies and gentlemen and if your website is not optimized for mobile devices (phones and tablets, for instance), you're behind the curve already. A ranking factor since 2015, mobile friendliness is not only here to stay, but can also impact your site's ranking.

To check this, head back into your Google Search Console and click on the "mobile usability" tab on the left-side menu.

Step 6: Look for Other Indexation Issues in GSC

You're going to be staying in Google Search Console for Step 6. To check for other/further indexation issues, you'll want to click on the "Coverage" page on the left-side menu of your GSC. This page will provide you with insights as to whether you have any coverage errors or excluded pages along with any pages that may have warnings.

Some common GSC errors you may come across include:

- Pages that have a "noindex" attribute, but that also appear in your sitemap.
- Pages that are blocked from being crawled in your robots.txt file but that are in your sitemap.
- 404 pages that have been submitted in your sitemap.

During this stage, you can also check again to see if your site is indexed by clicking on "Google Index" on the left side menu followed by "Index Status".

Again, for those not using GSC (but why not?!), you can verify that your site is indexed by typing:

Site:pendragonconsultingllc.com (only make sure to use *your* URL and not mine here)

If you find that your site is not actually indexed, this means that you have *no organic traffic* AND that you are not ranking. At all. It's that serious.

In many cases, this is a result of a rogue x-robots-tag HTTP header. Check out this article for help with troubleshooting that particular issue:

https://yoast.com/x-robots-tag-play/

If you hop back over to your SEMRush site audit (or Ahrefs if that's where you've run it), you can also see a breakdown of site coverage there as well. By checking to see the number of internal pages you can compare this to see how many pages were indexed on your GSC.

For example, if you have 83 internal pages but only 76 of them are indexed, this could indicate there's an issue somewhere. The exception would be if those pages are in fact marked as "noindex". If you do find issues, you'll want to get to the bottom of *why* those pages are not indexed by digging a bit deeper.

Step 7: The User Experience (UX)

Okay, we've talked about Google's algorithm update heading our way, the Page Experience. This update is making the ***user experience*** a ranking factor. That means that if your website does not provide users with an optimal experience, your website may very well end up downranked.

Some things to take into consideration when planning for this algorithm update include:

- Mobile friendliness
- Site speed
- Core web vitals

    - Largest contentful paint (i.e. load speed)
    - First input delay (i.e. responsiveness and user feel)
    - Cumulative layout shift (i.e. visual stability & layout shift of visible content)

Looking for an easy way to audit these? Go on back to your GSC and open the "enhancements" tab. From there you'll be able to see both mobile and desktop versions of the reports which will give you insight into any issues that may exist in relation to "poor" URLs.

Step 8: On-Site Checkup

If you get stuck through here, you can always refer back to the respective chapters on *on-site SEO*. In fact, as you go through, I'd encourage you to do so. Here are somethings you'll want to check:

- Heading tags
- Meta descriptions
- Keywords (are you using *the right* keywords?!)
- Image alt text/alt tags
- Title tags

- Internal linking
- Broken links
- Plagiarism/duplicate content
- Word count

There are a lot of tools out there that can help you streamline this process. SEMRush, Ahrefs and many more offer free solutions for this. In fact, if you query Google with something like "free SEO audit" you'll find a bevy of tools to use. Bear in mind that these are great for on-site SEO specifically, and not so much for off-site SEO.

Pages on your site that are not linked to from any other page are known as orphan pages. Yet another item that can ultimately downrank your site's ranking. Using the SEMRush Site Audit you generated in step one, you can also easily identify pages that are not being linked to. Easy solution here... go back through your site and link to the page in question.

A great tool to check for broken links is the Broken Link Checker: www.brokenlinkcheck.com. You can even get their Chrome extension to keep continuous track of whether you have any broken links.

Google HATES duplicate content, and you will get a slap on the wrist for it. Google's Panda update places emphasis on not having duplicate content. To find potential duplicate content issues with your website, you can use a tool called Copyscape (https://www.copyscape.com/). Chances are high that if you're looking at your home page you may have some duplicate content out there, like a short about on various directory listings or social pages. Those *short* bursts of text aren't necessarily anything to worry about unless someone has copied your work and/or scraped an entire blog. If someone has copied your work, make sure that they link back to your original work, ideally with a rel="canonical" link).

Word count is just as important. If your page has a low word count, you will not find favor in Google's eyes. This is because these pages provide little to no value and often struggle to rank. If you flip back to the section on *on-site SEO*, you'll see that the ideal word count is a minimum of 300 words, but certainly no less than 200 words. However, you should still aim for higher. I recommend 600+ words, but the more words, the better off you are as it provides more value and that's the end goal. You can check your word count here: https://wordcounter.net/website-word-count.

Step 9: Sitemap

Don't skip this... XML sitemaps make it easier for search bots to crawl your website and index the pages accordingly. A sitemap will tell the search engines:

- The location of a page on your website.
- Frequency it's updated.
- The importance of the page.
- When it was last updated.
- How it relates to other pages.

Without a sitemap, Google may conclude that your site has duplicate content, which again, could end up hurting your SEO.

Here's a free tool to help you build (and submit to the search engines) your XML sitemap:

https://www.xml-sitemaps.com/

Step 10: Redirects

If you've ended up changing your page title, your slug may have changed. If you've removed content from your website that you were previously linking to, this could cause your readers to link to content that doesn't exist. Can you see where we're going? In addition to this affecting the UX, you can also expect it to affect your SEO - especially after Google's Page Experience update.

In SEMRush's Site Audit report you can find a bunch of information on the temporary redirects, redirect chains & loops.

Step 11: Be on the Lookout for Toxic/Poor Quality Links

Remember in the beginning of this chapter I mentioned the tool Majestic? Here's where you'll want to use that.

Not all links will help you rank higher. Go ahead and say that again. Not all links will help you rank higher. SEMRush has a backlink audit tool (again with their 7-day free trial) or you can use Moz's Link Explorer tool (10 free queries per month).

Step 12: Structured Data Errors

To recap, schema markup is the same as structured data and it is a code that can be included on your website. This code can help search engines better understand what your site is all about so that it indexes you appropriately.

Now, you'll find that many will recommend using Google's Structured Data Testing Tool. In the past, we have recommended that as well. However, Google has announced that they are getting rid of this tool and are replacing it with the Rich Results Test, which is now officially out of beta.

> **This tool is being shut down**
>
> The Structured Data Testing Tool is being deprecated. For validating structured data for Google Search, Google now recommends using the Rich Results Test for more accurate and actionable feedback. For more information on this deprecation, read our blog post.
>
> DISMISS   **TRY RICH RESULTS TEST**

If you have structured data on your site, you may want to run it through this tool to check whether there are any errors.

Some examples of what may benefit from structured data/ schema markup include:

- Reviews
- Product information
- Events

If you do find errors in your structured data, this guide is an excellent resource:

https://structuredseo.com/how-to-fix-schema-markup-errors-using-googles-structured-data-tool/

Step 13: Organic Search Traffic

For this step, you'll want to open up your Google Analytics. Once you're in there, go ahead and click on "Acquisitions"

→Overview → Organic Search.

In here, you'll be able to see whether your *organic* search has improved. If you notice a *decrease* in the amount of search traffic, you'll want to go through and identify *why*.

Did the decrease occur during a specific timeframe - such as Christmas? Did you make significant changes to your website during that time?

Step 14: Competitor Analysis

This is where you want to take a look at which websites are hold the top-ranking spots for Google Search results on the keywords you'd like to rank for. Take a good look at those pages that are ranking. If let's say the top 5 are all similar, but your content is different, you may want to consider reworking your content.

I also like to use SurferSEO for this step. They have a Chrome extension that you can download for free called KeywordSurfer. When you type in your search term in Google, it shows up with a number of items, including a comparison of the top ranked sites and their links, the page's word count, etc. This is a great starting point.

You'll want to keep digging though beyond the results from KeywordSurfer to really see what they're doing and how you can improve your content.

Next Steps

Now that you've identified issues with your site through this audit, you'll want to take action. The longer you delay on correcting these issues, the longer you'll be stuck in a lower ranking position. The SEO audit can help you create an effective strategy for implementation. Many of these items could easily be done yourself, but if you find yourself needing some support, you can always reach out to a developer (or Pendragon Consulting → shameless plug) to assist with the gaps in what you're not able to accomplish yourself.

14 Things That Can Hurt Your Site Rankings

You are busy creating lots of low quality links to your site

- Look for site messages under Search Console, run Semrush Backlink Audit.
- Try to remove low quality links by outreaching the site owner or disavowing them as a last resort.

You have violated copyright knowingly or unknowingly

- Check your URL in the Google Transparency Report.
- Remove the pages that are inviting copyright violation asap.

You have recently changed the internal linking

- Download the data and cross-check from GSC.
- Fix all the 404's if you find them.

Your site has suddenly become unsafe

- Visit GSC and check for any message from Google.
- Google will suggest the steps you need to take.

You have lots of links pointing to other sites

- Check GSC for messages about "Unnatural links from your website".
- Remove all the unnatural links.

Your site has duplicate content

- Use Semrush Site Audit tool.
- Implement 301 redirects, rel=canonical and rel=noindex where needed.

Your site is not mobile friendly

- Take the Google mobile-friendly test.
- Google will suggest the changes you need to implement.

Google has made a recent update to its ranking algorithm

- Keep a watch on the official Google Webmasters Blog.
- Subscribe to reputed blogs in the SEO industry to learn tips from experts.

You have recently made changes in content

- Use OnWebChange that notifies you about any changes in the design or content.
- Optimize new content for SEO.

There is a rise in competition

- Run a Google search and identify your competitors.
- Conduct a competitive analysis and fix gaps in your strategy.

Google has made a recent update

- Create a Google alert for updates.
- Read reputed blogs in the SEO industry for details and tips.

You have recently updated your title or meta tags

- Export a list of all landing pages from GA, use Screaming Frog to check the new meta tags.
- Rewrite them and include the missing keywords.

Your site has bad redirects

- Run the Site Audit tool> "Redirect chains and loops".
- Create an alternate URL for every new redirect and navigate users to a new page that has the same/ even better content.

Your site is getting lots of low-quality traffic

- Run a check in Finteza.
- Find websites that are referring low-quality traffic, remove your links/ads from them.

How NOT to Kill Your SEO While Rebranding Your Company

Whatever reason you've decided to rebrand your company, it's never just as simple as just doing it. Quite a bit goes into rebranding and too often, SEO is often under accounted for. Where exactly does SEO fit into rebranding? The last thing you want is to have worked so hard at SEO only to lose all that progress after a name change.

With a little research and a healthy dose of effort, decreased SEO rankings doesn't have to be a biproduct of your rebranding efforts.

*Disclaimer: You will likely notice a slight decrease in your SEO after you've rebranded, but if you take the necessary steps, you shouldn't suffer a **tremendous** loss in SEO.*

6 Steps to Maintaining SEO When Rebranding

1. Keep Your Original Domain Name - If Possible
2. Maintain Existing Content
3. Refrain from Deleting Your Old Website Right Away
4. Prepare Your 301 Redirects
5. Update Your Citations and Backlinks
6. Ensure Your New Site is Mobile Friendly

Keep Your Original Domain Name - If Possible

It may not always be feasible, but to really give yourself the best possible start to rebranding while maintaining your SEO try to keep the same domain name (URL of your website). More often than not though, when a company seeks to rebrand, the name is the most common change. So, maintaining the same domain may not always be possible.

If you are able to however, there may be minimal to no change to your SEO or Domain Authority (DA).

Maintain Existing Content

You've likely been working on the content of your website for a while ensuring that you're hitting on those valuable keywords/key phrases to show up in search engines. If you're going with a new website all together and/or a new domain, try to salvage as much of the content on your website to preserve those keywords stashed in your website's content and <u>blogs</u>.

This is particularly valuable for both companies that are and are not changing domains. For companies that decide to use the same domain but perhaps are considering redoing their website, you should also try to salvage as much of the content on your website as well.

Refrain from Deleting Your Old Website Right Away

If you are going to use a new domain for your rebranding, you'll want to leave your old website up for at least a few days after your new website launches. The reason for leaving your old website up for at least a few days (or weeks preferably) is because it can potentially take the servers several days to recognize new IP addresses. This means that if you were to take down your old website as soon as your new website launches you could potentially ruin your hard work.

Prepare Your 301 Redirects

To keep both users and search engines happy, you'll need to <u>redirect</u> all of the pages from your old website to the most relevant/similar page on your new website. This can all be setup and ready to go when your new website goes live without officially going live until your website does.

If your old site and your new site both have the same pages and similar URL structure, this process could be as simple as adding a couple lines of code to simply reroute the pages. For those with different pages and/or URL structure, this process may be a bit more time consuming.

These 301 redirects are pretty important and can often be overlooked. The search engines could end up downranking your websites if your 301 redirects aren't in place or working properly on top of creating a poor user experience. Here's another vital reason for 301 redirects that many business owners simply don't take into account: backlinks. If your website has been around for a little while and/or you've spent any time or money on backlinks to boost the authority of your website, those 301 redirects can redirect any traffic to your new page.

Update Your Citations and Backlinks

<u>Local SEO</u> can be critical to ranking higher in your local area and consists of building citations (listings) in directories

to help you rank higher in the search engines local listings as well as to drive more traffic to your business. When rebranding, you'll want to ensure that you're updating all of those citations to ensure your company's NAPs (name, address and phone number) are accurate. Search engines may downrank you if they don't know which name or contact information is accurate.

Backlinks obtained through white hat methods should be preserved as best as possible to avoid any drop in SEO. In addition to creating 301 redirects, you should reach out to webmasters on any sites that you may have a backlink from to get any links updated to your current page to maintain your backlinks.

Ensure Your New Website is Mobile Friendly

All you have to do is look at your analytics or insights to see that the majority of traffic to your website and social accounts come from mobile devices. The search engines know this and are placing more value in websites that are optimized for mobile devices. It's not just about ensuring things are aesthetically pleasing on the mobile version of your website, but also that you are working to improve the user experience through things like faster load times, etc.

Rebranding is like putting together a puzzle. There are lots of pieces, but each piece to the puzzle is just as important. Don't be afraid to rebrand, just make sure that you've done your homework and are doing as much as you can to preserve the SEO and search engine rankings you've worked so hard to establish. Remember to be realistic as well. Go into the process knowing that there will likely be some drop in your domain authority and SEO to avoid disappointment but remember there are ways to reduce the impact.

Afterword

SEO is an essential part of your online success. It can have *significant* impact on your business when done correctly and should not be skipped over or half done. Your competitors are out there optimizing their sites and content. If you're not optimizing, you're already behind the curve and may even be almost non-existent in terms of ranking.

I sincerely hope that this book provided you with a basic understanding of what SEO is and how to get started. Please bear in mind that this book was made for those just starting out and is not meant to provide advanced level information or to make you an expert.

This book is meant to be a living document. This means that you can expect a new edition to be released annually. There are algorithm updates that happen and impact SEO all the time. If you notice anything that's missing from this book, that you feel should be expanded on or just want to send a quick note, drop us a line:

www.pendragonconsultingllc.com/contact

I wish you all much success on your SEO journey and don't forget to check out my other books on Facebook Advertising and Content Marketing!

Additional Resources

Beginner's Guide to Facebook Group:

https://www.facebook.com/groups/beginnersguidetoseo

FREE Resources:

https://beginnersguidetocontentmarketing.com/seo

Pendragon Consulting, LLC:

www.pendragonconsultingllc.com

The Beginner's Guide to Marketing Podcast:

https://anchor.fm/jessica-ainsworth

The Beginner's Guide to Marketing:

https://www.beginnersguidetomarketing.com/

Tools to Consider (In Order of Appearance)

Google Keyword Planner:

https://ads.google.com/home/tools/keyword-planner/

Google AdWords:

https://ads.google.com/home/#!/

Google Trends:

https://trends.google.com/trends/?geo=US

Moz Keyword Explorer:

https://moz.com/explorer

Surfer's Keyword Surfer (Chrome plugin):

https://surferseo.com/keyword-surfer-extension/

Higher Intent Keywords:

https://www.adamriemer.me/50-modifiers-boost-seo-drive-sales/

TinyPNG:

https://tinypng.com/

Mention - Keep an eye on who is mentioning your brand online:

https://mention.com/en/

CopyScape - plagiarism checker:

https://www.copyscape.com/

SEMrush:

https://www.semrush.com

Ahrefs:

https://ahrefs.com/

Spyfu:

https://www.spyfu.com/

BrightLocal - to help with your Local SEO:

https://www.brightlocal.com/

PageSpeed Insight tool - owned by Google:

https://developers.google.com/speed/pagespeed/insights/

CrazyEgg's article on speeding up your website:

https://www.crazyegg.com/blog/speed-up-your-website/

Varvy - for help with Javascript on HTML sites:

https://varvy.com/pagespeed/defer-loading-javascript.html

Web Page Test - to test your time to first byte (TTFB):

https://www.webpagetest.org/

Robots Testing Tool - A Google tool that allows you to test your robots.txt file:

https://www.google.com/webmasters/tools/robots-testing-tool

XML Sitemap Generator:

https://www.xml-sitemaps.com/

Aleyda Solis's site for helping with hreflangs:

https://www.aleydasolis.com/english/international-seo-tools/hreflang-tags-generator/

Broken Link Checker:

https://www.brokenlinkcheck.com/

Down for everyone - a website to check whether your website is down for just you or for everyone:

https://downforeveryoneorjustme.com/

Google's Webmaster Search Central Help Community:

https://support.google.com/webmasters/community/?hl=en&gpf=%23!forum%2Fwebmasters

Screaming Frog - SEO tool:

https://www.screamingfrog.co.uk/seo-spider/

Google Search Console:

https://search.google.com/search-console/about

Google Analytics:

https://analytics.google.com/analytics/web/

Google's Structured Data Testing Tool:

https://search.google.com/structured-data/testing-tool/u/0/

Web Page Word Counter:

https://wordcounter.net/website-word-count

Majestic:

https://majestic.com

Rank Ranger:

https://www.rankranger.com

Blogs to Check Out

HubSpot:

https://blog.hubspot.com/marketing

Pendragon Consulting:

https://www.pendragonconsultingllc.com/blog

Precision Legal Marketing:

https://precisionlegalmarketing.com/blog/

Rank Ranger:

https://www.rankranger.com/blog

Search Engine Journal:

https://www.searchenginejournal.com/

Search Engine Land:

https://searchengineland.com/library/channel/seo

SEMrush:

https://www.semrush.com/blog/

BONUS

If you've made it this far, you're awesome :D Here's a bonus resource! This site lists out 150+ guest posting sites to apply to :

https://www.advancedwebranking.com/blog/150-sites-to-guest-post/

Glossary

404 - HTTP status code that means that the webpage a visitor is trying to access is unavailable or sometimes does not exist.

301 Redirect - Used to indicate the permanent moving of a web page. For example, you can ask the server to redirect visitors from the old URL to a new location — using a 301 redirect.

302 Redirect - Used to indicate that a webpage has moved temporarily.

Alt-text - Used in a HTML code to describe a visual element (usually a photo) on a webpage.

Anchor Text - A clickable text a user clicks to move from one document or webpage destination to another.

Backlink - A link created when one website connects to another.

Blackhat SEO - A practice that goes against search engine guidelines aimed at increasing a webpage's search ranking.

Brand Awareness - Ability of a customer to identify a brand by name, visually or through a message.

Brand Recognition - Extent to which a customer can recognize a brand and differentiate it with other brands.

Branded Keyword - Keyword/search term that contains the companies name.

Canonicalization - A way of telling a search engine that a specific URL is the master copy of a page and not a duplicate version.

Competitor Research - An assessment targeting major competitors of a business, looking at their strength and weaknesses.

CPC (*Cost Per Click*) - The amount paid per click on a pay per click ad - such as Google AdWords.

Crawl Error - An error that occurs while search bots try to reach/crawl a page of your site but fails.

Dofollow - A link to another website that allows both people and search engines to follow the link to the other website. A dofollow link is ideal as it provides SEO value.

Domain - URLs that people type on a browser to find a website.

Domain Authority (*DA*) - This is a metric that is used to gauge how well a website will rank on search engine results page (SERP).

Favicon - An icon associated with a web page, brand and/or website.

Google AdWords - An advertising platform by Google enabling advertisers to bid on certain words in order to rank in a top position/page one in order to reach their potential customers in a timelier manner.

Google Analytics - Web analytic tool by google that provides information about a website and visitor traffic.

Google My Business (*GMB*) - A tool for businesses created by Google that helps organizations manage their web presence on google including maps and searches.

Google Search Console (*GSC*) - A console provided for free by google to better understand how a website is performing in Google's search results.

Heading Tag - HTML tag used to indicate the headings and subheadings of a webpage.

Hosting - Process of a hosting provider allocating space on a web server for websites to store their files.

Hreflang - A HTML tag used to specify the language and geographical targets of a website.

Inbound Links - Links from one site (a site other than your own) directing to a page on your site.

Indexation - The process of adding webpages into search engine databases after search bots have crawled your website.

Infographic - Combination of pictures and words to be able to communicate to a target audience in a simplified manner.

Internal Link - Hyperlinks that redirect a webpage to another webpage on the same domain.

Keyword Research - This is the process of identifying key words and phrases that people use while conducting searches which can help business owners in creating targeted content.

Landing Page - A page where a user first gets to when they open a webpage.

Local SEO - A practice that involves optimizing a website to be more visible on searches on google in a geographical area.

Long-Tail Keyword - More specific and targeted key word phrases that consist of lower search volumes AND a lower competition score.

Markup - A form of microdata when added to a webpage creates an enhanced description which appear in search results.

Meta Description - HTML element that summarizes a page's content. This is the content that typically appears under a search result when querying Google, for instance.

Meta Tag - Part of HTML code that tell search engines about a website's content.

NAP (*Name, Address, Phone Number*) - This entails a business's contact information, which search engines take into account when determining which companies to show first in geo targeted searches (i.e. local SEO).

Negative SEO - Malicious act aimed at reducing a competitor's ranking by tactics such as building spam links, sending fake link removal requests and writing fake reviews.

Nofollow - A nofollow link tells search engines that they should ignore the link in question and not to assign any SEO value to it.

Off-Site SEO - Involves actions taken *off* of the website to improve search results ranking.

On-Site SEO - Process of optimizing individual pages content *on your* website to be able to rank better on search and drive relevant traffic.

Page Experience - Google's new ranking algorithm to be used to judge how users perceive their experience while visiting a webpage (set to be released in early 2021).

Page Speed - Time taken for a webpage to load.

Page Title - The headline that shows the title of a webpage.

PPC (*Pay Per Click*) - A form of paid advertising in which advertisers can rank in a top position by paying each time a person clicks on their advertisement.

Robots.txt - A text file that tells search engine which search bots can or cannot access your site.

ROI (*Return On Investment*) - Process of calculating the gain received from an investment made over the cost of investment.

Schema.org - A collaboration between major search engines such as Google, Microsoft, Yahoo! and Yandex that contains shared vocabularies associated with a set of properties.

SEM (*Search Engine Marketing*) - An internet marketing strategy to gain website traffic by purchasing Ads on search engines (Google AdWords for example).

SEO (*Search Engine Optimization*) - The practice of understanding what users are searching for online - to increase traffic to your website, and also expose your brand to potential target audience when they search online using different search engines.

SEO Audit - Process of analyzing a website to indicate its health in visibility in search engine rankings.

SERP (*Search Engine Results Page*) - Web page results that show when a user queries a search engine.

Site Speed - Time taken for a webpage to load.

Sitemap - A list of content giving an overview of the pages within a specific website.

Spam Score - An online checker created by MOZ to give a percentage of whether a website has similar features of webpages banned or penalized by google.

Structured Data - Standardized way to organize information about a web page and to communicate it within that organized structure to help search engines better understand the webpage content.

Technical SEO - Optimizations that make a website crawlable, fast and secure to improve search visibility. Examples include hreflang, robots.txt, sitemaps, etc.

Thought Leader - Individuals or company who are known authorities in their field of expertise.

URL (*Uniform Resource Locator*) - Location of a page, file, or specific webpage on the internet.

User Experience (*UX*) - How a person feels while interacting with a particular website or online platform. Various metrics are used to determine whether a website is providing an optimal user experience.

User Intent - States the goal a user aims to achieve when conducting a search query on a search engine.

Webmaster - A person responsible for handling websites.

Whitehat SEO - Practice of using approved search engine guidelines, techniques, and tactics.

Pendragon Consulting

Your Partner in Expanding the Foregrounds of Digital Marketing Excellence

The story of digital marketing efficacy always starts with an effective strategy. Without a plan, you might as well be aimlessly targeting advertisements that lead to no results.

This is where Pendragon Consulting comes in. A strong penchant for research enables us to create that game plan and give you a strategy that will generate phenomenal results while also improving user engagement.

Who Is Pendragon Consulting?

Results-driven and research-focused, Pendragon Consulting is a digital marketing agency helping businesses in the service industry gauge and optimize their online presence. We offer our clients a comprehensive range of digital marketing services that encompass our varying expertise.

We understand that your business deserves a stable online presence that delivers results. You put thought into the services you provide and the products you sell; so we put in the effort to make sure your efforts reach the right audience and gain you traction that improves your bottom line.

www.PendragonConsultingLLC.com
hello@pendragonconsultingllc.com

Author Bio

Jessica Ainsworth, Founder of <u>Pendragon Consulting, LLC</u>, a digital marketing agency based out of Maryland, is focused on helping businesses expand their reach into new pools of potential customers. She has a strong background in research and analytics and has turned that into a passion for marketing. Author of *The Beginner's Guide to Facebook Advertising: Create Impactful Ads and Increase Your Return on Investment* and *The Beginner's Guide to Content Marketing: How to Drive Traffic, Provide Value and Increase Revenue*, Jessica loves teaching small businesses how to stand on their own two feet to remain competitive without having to pay an agency to do it for them (unless they want to - in which case, give Pendragon a call).

Former intelligence analyst and total nerd, Jessica has a special fondness for research and analytics. Having a strong background in analytics, marketing seemed like an almost natural career transition. She is a veteran, author, marketing professional, philanthropist and board member at 22 March for Life, a veteran suicide prevention organization.

Connect with Jessica on LinkedIn!

LinkedIn personal: https://www.linkedin.com/in/jessica-ains-3b3194187/

Made in the USA
Columbia, SC
08 June 2022